ILLITERACY:
A National Dilemma

Other Books by David Harman

Adult Illiteracy in the United States
Learning to be Parents: Principles, Programs, Methods
Functional Education for Family Life Planning
Community Fundamental Education

DAVID HARMAN

Illiteracy
A National Dilemma

C A M B R I D G E
The Adult Education Company
NEW YORK · TORONTO

Dedicated to the memory of

Jerrold R. Zacharias

Cherished friend and wise mentor,
who has had a central impact on educational thought
and practice over the past decades.
As a principal architect of the modern
curriculum-reform movement,
following a distinguished career as a physicist,
he pioneered new approaches to curriculum development
and influenced a generation of educators.
For Jerrold no challenge was too daunting,
no problem insurmountable. Before tackling any issue
he insisted on understanding it thoroughly,
firmly believing that the deeper the knowledge,
the easier it would be to find good solutions.
This book is offered in that spirit.

MANUFACTURED IN THE UNITED STATES OF AMERICA

ISBN 0-8428-2227-5

10 9 8 7 6 5 4 3 2 1

Cover and interior design by Jacqueline Schuman

CONTENTS

v

1

What Is Literacy?

In 1970, a few months after the first moon walk, United States Commissioner of Education James Allen, Jr., proclaimed the "right to read." If the United States could achieve the giant step of putting a man on the moon, he declared, the relatively simple problem of teaching the earthbound to read was certainly no longer beyond us. The attainment of universal literacy was to be the "moonshot for the seventies." Nearly two decades after this clarion call, the goal is as distant as ever.

Wars have been declared against illiteracy, campaigns have been launched, battles fought against this "scourge." Reports that tens of millions of Americans are illiterate excite waves of indignation, excoriations of the school system, and demands for prompt redress and rectification. Hundreds of millions of dollars are spent annually on the teaching of reading, on research, on the production of textbooks, and on the training of teachers—and the problem persists. Institutes are set up, teams are formed, volunteers are organized—and reports continue to pour in on the appalling number of adults who can't read. The problem isn't confined to school dropouts and the disadvantaged members of minority groups, although they account for the greatest number of illiterates; more and more working members of mainstream America are found to be either totally illiterate or unable to read at the level presumably required by their job or their position in society.

The recognition that universal literacy is a social and cultural imperative, while relatively new in historical terms, is nonetheless centuries old. Universal compulsory schooling, a nineteenth-century development that until quite recently was the domain of only some countries, has by now been adopted, if not implemented, internationally. And yet, as people everywhere strive to achieve fully literate societies, their efforts seem to be perpetually obstructed.

There are many who believe that all that is required to eradicate illiteracy is a lot of money, an army of instructors, some textbooks and manuals. Advocates of this approach see illiteracy in highly simplistic terms, a "mere" inability to read and write that can be easily rectified through the conduct of lightning war. They point to literacy campaigns that have been conducted in other lands as examples of the kind of concerted action that could be taken. They neglect, in their enthusiasm for rapid results, to look at the meager achievements most of those campaigns have made. They arrogantly sweep aside efforts to learn more about both literacy and the processes of its acquisition, claiming that "enough is known; all that is necessary is action."

Well meaning as such an approach may be, it is wrong in most of its positions. Illiteracy is not a simple "disease"—it is a complicated manifestation of multiple causes and is deeply rooted in both culture and social dynamic. Literacy is not the simple ability to read and write—it is a highly complex concept that derives its definition from different conditions among different groups at different times. It is not one and the same for all people, but has as many different faces as there are groups and communities. Indeed, a nation that prides itself on its pluralism cannot at the same time aspire to one uniform definition of literacy. Attempts to teach literacy without due regard for the values and motives of the learners are doomed to failure. Teaching—particularly the teaching of adults—is an art and a science. Well-meaning but untrained instructors are for the most part ill equipped to undertake it.

The problem is not with the schools, or with the teachers, or with the methods of teaching, or with the training of literacy volunteers, or with the willingness or unwillingness of adult illiterates to seek help.

The problem is in the nature of literacy itself.

It is not insoluble, but the solution must rise from the nature of the problem. To combat illiteracy, we need to answer the question, what is literacy?

Defining Literacy

Most of the world's population is illiterate. Some of the illiterates are young children who have not yet learned how to read. Others, irrespective of age, were never taught. Yet others, despite having attended schools, either did not succeed in acquiring adequate reading skills or lost them through lack of use. Some people who read well enough to "get by" find their reading skills are inadequate when they find themselves in a new situation; others who can't read at all are able to act as though they can. People who are regarded as literate by one standard are considered illiterate by another.

Nearly two decades after Allen's clarion call, the realization of "the right to read" is as distant as it ever was.

The attempt to define literacy is like a walk to the horizon: as one walks toward it, it continuously recedes. Similarly, as groups of people achieve the skills formerly defined as literacy, altered circumstances often render definitions obsolete. New definitions replace the old ones as new goals are set. People considered literate by a previous yardstick are now regarded as illiterate.

The term *functional literacy,* invented to distinguish advanced concepts of literacy, has itself become a variable, lending itself to constant redefinition.

Literacy Skills

When we talk of teaching, what exactly are the skills that we seek to inculcate? What is this quality that so many people are said to lack to their own and society's detriment?

At its simplest, literacy refers to reading and writing abilities— the skill of associating sounds with the written symbols that represent them, and then connecting those symbols to form words, sentences, and whole texts. The terms *reading* and *writing,* which form the core of literacy, in fact establish very little. They do not, for instance, convey any notion of the content or uses of what is read or written.

If oral language constitutes the primary mode of human communication, then literacy is its logical extension: the representation of language through written symbols that maintain their meaning over time and space. Literacy makes it possible to record language both in order to extend the range of communication and to preserve speech.

Reading and writing, then, together constitute the skill of manipulating written forms of language—the adeptness at expressing language in writing on the one hand, and of extracting meaning from written representations of language on the other.

Once reading and writing have been acquired, what one applies them to and how they are used—that is, what people actually read and write—is a matter decided partly by the society and partly by the individual. Societies set expectations for their members in regard to many aspects of life, including the use of literacy skills. Some societies determine that certain texts should be read by all members; the Bible, for example, must be read by all members of certain religious groups. Other written materials might be designated as requirements for certain positions and occupations within the society: doctors, lawyers, and teachers are expected to be conversant with their professional journals, landlords and tenants with the leases they sign, consumers with labels and warranties, students with their homework assignments. Such expectations determine more specific definitions of literacy.

Outside of these expectations, the questions of whether or not to read, what to read, and when to read are determined by individuals. In societies that place a high premium on reading, those who chose not to read, or cannot do so, are apt to find themselves on the social fringes. In groups that attach no importance at all to literacy, illiterate persons will not be socially disadvantaged, but groups as a whole will suffer deprivation. For example, it is probably no accident that non-literate societies are largely found in the less-developed corners of the globe and not in advanced countries.

Because literacy, in broad terms, is a concept far greater than the mere technical ability to cope with letters, any attempt to define it must be done in a cultural context. In 1956 William Gray proposed an omnibus definition: "A person is functionally literate when he has acquired the knowledge and skills in reading and writing which enable him to engage effectively in all those activities in which literacy is normally assumed in his cultural group."[1] Literacy is neither neutral nor universal. It is subjective and particular.

Definitions of literacy need to be "situation specific": as each group has unique attributes that serve to define literacy for members into words, he or she is technically a reader. Beyond that point the main difference between reading levels is a matter of comprehension. Comprehension, in turn, requires vocabulary as well as enough information to provide a context for what is being read. The greater one's command of a language, presumably, the greater will be one's comprehension.

The various formulas designed to measure reading level are based on the length and structure of words rather than the words themselves. *Identifiable* has two syllables more than *lawrencium* but is an easier word to understand and requires less specialized knowledge in a particular field. Vocabulary, which provides the key to understanding texts, accumulates in direct relation to the involvements of the individual. A student's vocabulary is developed mainly through the subjects studied, although external associations also have an important influence. Following graduation, one's occupation, interests and pursuits, family, and community all contribute to its further growth, bringing an increasing range of written materials into one's purview. The tests that establish reading level ability should therefore be different for seventeen-year-olds than for adults: while the skill being examined is the same and the emphasis is still on comprehension, the materials included in tests ought to differ significantly.

Application to Adults

It is questionable whether the measure of reading ability made during school attendance ought to be regarded as valid throughout adult life. There is room for the creation of a new measure that would be more appropriate for adults and would more accurately describe an individual's reading skills over the years following graduation.

One attempt to provide such a measure was made by the University of Texas Adult Proficiency Level (APL) study, published in 1975. The study identified 65 reading- and writing-related tasks that its designers felt adult Americans should be able to perform, such as reading job notices, filling out job application forms, addressing envelopes, and reading road signs. Instead of analyzing each of the tasks as to its appropriate grade level, the researchers chose to derive a three-stage ladder of adult performance abilities from the tasks that had been selected. This research did more than merely replace one series of measurements with another; it established a standard of measurement designed specifically for adults.

The matter of measuring literacy remains problematic. Despite their drawbacks, grade levels continue to be used as the basic unit of literary measurement.

Functional Literacy

Functional literacy is a complex notion that deviates substantially from conventional definitions of literacy. While technical reading skills are considered in measuring functional literacy, they constitute only one of its components. Literacy can only properly exist when the reading and writing abilities are complemented by vocabulary and knowledge.

During the 1960s a notion gained currency that functional literacy was simply a higher-level reading ability, at a standard above that of a fourth-grade level. Reading at a level less than that, it was argued, made it virtually impossible to read texts of any substance and, consequently, resulted in almost total illiteracy. Researchers have sought, since that time, to identify a level that would form the benchmark of functionality and have variously proposed standards ranging from a fourth- to a twelfth-grade level. This search has almost become a modern-day quest for the Holy Grail. It is probably the case that there is no single standard that can serve to identify a base level of functional literacy, as functional literacy is such an amorphous and variable concept. As the National Institute of Education noted in 1979: "What literacy means in performance terms in a developed economy is not certain. There simply isn't a lot of information on levels and kinds of reading and writing that are needed by a second grader, a high school vocational student, a senior at a prestigious university, or a farmer, a bureaucrat, or a researcher."

The situation is probably even more complex. Actual requirements regarding reading are influenced by one's status, occupation, and interests, but are also circumscribed by one's environment.

Occupational Issues
Assume for a moment that it has been found that to be an effective farmer in Iowa one ought to be reading at a ninth-grade level. That does not necessarily mean that all farmers should be able to read at

8

that standard to be properly functional. It is quite likely that in another locale, where the nature of farming is different, a sixth-grade level is all that is needed, while in yet another, from a purely functional point of view, literacy is not required at all. Successful farming in each of these situations is defined differently and has different literacy content. Bringing the farmers in the latter two areas up to a ninth-grade level of competence—if that were possible—would probably not improve their functioning as farmers at all, as the incremental reading ability may not have any real applications. If all farmers were to move to Iowa, there would be some logic in such an instructional effort, but since they will remain functioning in their own environments, it would be a wasted and most likely nonproductive undertaking. Although this is but a hypothetical example, it illustrates the difficulty in seeking a national or universal benchmark of functional literacy.

Functional literacy, even more than mechanical reading and writing skills, is a relative set of capabilities. It can only derive its real definition from actual conditions pertaining in a particular situation and does not lend itself to generalization. In arriving at definitions it should be borne in mind that possession of a certain level of reading ability is no guarantee that it will be put to use. Rather, what is more likely is that people will actively seek and attain those literacy levels that are dictated by their environments.

In abstract terms it can be said that individuals who cannot read at, say, a ninth-grade level have no access to certain materials, such as newspapers, some manuals, and a large body of literature. However, it is most often the case that people reading below a ninth-grade level live in environments that place no particular value on reading any of those materials, and others in such communities who can read at higher levels probably don't.

Personal and Social Issues

This notion is not a brief for the proposition that there is no literacy problem. There certainly is a severe problem, but it is not, alas, a simple one. It could, indeed, be argued that there are two literacy issues. The first is the one conventionally dealt with: the issue of personal literacy. It relates to those individuals whose reading abilities fall below some stipulated level. It would, in the terms put forth here, largely consist of people unable to read at the level that is actually determined by their environments as being necessary. Anecdotes abound about people who mask their reading deficiency through all sorts of subterfuge. Such individuals recognize that their abilities are below those that are normative in the communities of which they are members.

The second literacy issue is not individual but social and environmental. It pertains to communities in which literacy is not expected and its existence not rewarded. Within such societies individuals cannot properly develop literacy skills at levels that exceed the local definition. There are simply no outlets for the additional ability and it might, in fact, be looked at askance because it would be abnormal. In such situations the literacy challenge has to be cast in macro rather than micro terms: it is the community that must become literacy conscious and establish a definition of expectation for its members. Only then can the process of inculcating literacy to individuals commence with some assurance that skills will be acquired and put to use.

Mobility

Literate people often assume that literacy is a natural condition and that the lack of literacy abilities is tantamount to being diseased. But literate people tend to live and function in literate societies and might find it difficult to accept that other communities have different structures and place emphasis on different abilities.

When individuals move from a community in which literacy skills are not highly regarded to one in which they are, motivation to improve abilities soars. This happens because a person who was fully functional has been rendered nonfunctional in his or her new environment. Mobility allows people to move from one environment to another—from one set of social demands to another. The new set of demands determines a new set of attitudes, including, if the situation demands it, a new attitude toward literacy.

Environments also change. Such change is usually less dramatic and immediate than individual change. It often occurs over such lengthy spans of time that specific changes in literacy definitions take place in very small steps, often across rather than within generations.

It is not unlike the individual mobility pattern, but for obvious reasons it is more laborious.

It can be seen that not one uniform definition of functional literacy is appropriate for the entire country. Rather, there should be a plethora of definitions, each appropriate for a specific community at a particular time. Such definitions ought to reflect environmental norms, expectations regarding literacy, and objective conditions. In addition, functional literacy needs to be defined both for individuals and for communities. Working with one and not the other is working in the dark.

Literacy as a Value

There is a common tendency to view literacy in purely educational terms. If one is illiterate or functionally illiterate, there are thought to be gaps in one's education (usually considered to be synonymous with schooling) that require correction. However, illiteracy may be as much a sociocultural phenomenon as an educational one. The illiteracy problem is not created solely by the schools, and its solution does not rest entirely on their shoulders. Schools are not necessarily the source of the problem, and improvement of the schools is not necessarily the most appropriate strategy for change.

More than a set of skills, literacy is a value. Societies that place an important value on being literate actively seek to inculcate it and provide rewards to those who are literate. In other societies literacy is viewed as a less important value and is less avidly pursued. In such societies, even if literacy is firmly embedded in the schools curriculum, literacy cannot properly take hold.

2
Literacy in History

The biological-historical fact is that homo sapiens is a species which uses oral speech, manufactured by the mouth, to communicate. . . . He is not, by definition, a writer or reader. His use of speech . . . has been acquired by processes of natural selection operating over a million years. The habit of using written symbols to represent such speech is just a useful trick which has existed over too short a span of time to have been built into our genes, whether or not this may happen half a million years hence.[1]

Written language has always followed on the heels of spoken language—but never hard on its heels. It appears that in most cultures, at some point or another, it has been felt that language should be recorded. Quite obviously, when something is recorded by representing it with a symbol, a need arises for that symbol to be deciphered. Hence, reading and writing are intimately linked. One simply cannot exist without the other.

Origins of Literacy

The origins of reading and writing are ancient and obscure. Precisely which group devised the notion of committing language to symbols and at what point in its development this occurred is not known. Moreover, there is some controversy over the demarcation between random drawings and formalized symbols. Without doubt, however, the origins and evolution of writing systems form a major developmental step in the history of humankind.

As anthropologists Jack Goody and Ian Watt have remarked, "Looked at in the perspective of time, man's biological evolution shades into prehistory when he becomes a language-using animal; add writing, and history proper begins." "History proper," of course, relies heavily on written records, and recording is one of the main reasons for the evolution of writing systems.

People in different communities gradually arrived at the realization that mechanisms were necessary to enable them to record law and lore for transmission to their progeny. Otherwise, they surmised, it would not be possible to preserve their cultures and heritages. Goody and Watt point out that cultures naturally seek to transmit three things to succeeding generations: the land and natural resources that sustain subsistence, the normative patterns of behavior that define life style, and most important, the "range of meanings and attitudes which members of any society attach to their verbal symbols. . . . In short the Weltanschauung of every social group."[2] Anthropologist Ruth Benedict wrote that all groups of people have to devise the ways and means for transmitting their material and cultural possessions, as well as their modes of functioning, to future generations. For this purpose all groups have developed forms of education and the tools—methods—which enable that education to be effective. Such tools usually consist of verbal transmission and imitative behavior, and they often include some form of records using agreed-upon symbols that can be deciphered.

The symbols—essentially writing systems—serve two distinct purposes. First, they make it possible to maintain records, to commit thoughts and actions to writing so that they can exist across time and be available to future generations. Second, they serve as mnemonic devices, as aids to memory. By looking at a picture, or pictograph, or a set of symbols, individuals are enabled to associate them with the content they convey. The content itself, throughout much of human history, has been familiar to people, not new material.

These were the original purposes of writing. They served as a maintenance mechanism, allowing groups of people and cultures to preserve their heritage over time, providing some assurance that a culture would be sustained. While people were probably aware that changes occur, they most likely also felt that they ought to do the most they could to transfer everything possible, as accurately as possible.

Writing and recording, of course, span space as well as time. They make it possible for individuals who do not live in close proximity to communicate—to receive messages and transmit responses. Reading and writing can also be exclusionary—only those knowing the language and symbols can be participants.

Reading and writing systems rapidly became central in importance. It made it possible for people to exchange information and ideas, to expand horizons, without ever moving from one place. It made it possible for people to govern large tracts of land—to create and administer large empires and to command by "remote control." It was, indeed, a development so radical that it irrevocably altered the course of human history.

Literacy and Faith

The written word has been important in the propagation of dogmas. The spread of monotheistic religions—first Judaism, then Christianity, and finally Islam—was made possible by the use of written texts. By no means a rapid development, more than a millennium elapsed in this process. For all three religions the ability to commit words to writing was an essential ingredient in their becoming widely disseminated and adopted. The Old Testament, the New Testament, and the Koran are indeed, the quintessential example of the great power of the written word. Throughout most of medieval and early modern history they were to affect most aspects of life and also the spread of literacy itself.

The Middle Ages
Though direct access to the Scriptures could only be gained by reading, throughout the Middle Ages the literate formed only a tiny elite. The masses were kept illiterate by design as much as by circumstance. Elites of the Roman Catholic Church—which had spread its hegemony throughout Europe—firmly believed that it was their function to serve as mediators of God's word to the people and, indeed, that giving the populace direct access by inculcating reading skills might be dangerous and lead to sedition. Clearly, although not often stated explicitly, mass literacy could have brought about an erosion in the virtually absolute authority exercised by the clergy. Since the clergy

fully understood the power of the written word, it is not surprising that they chose not to share power too broadly.

Similarly, and in parallel, the secular governing cliques also saw no purpose in espousing mass education and the spread of literacy. Influenced by the Church and themselves desirous of confining the distribution of documents and use of writing to their own class, secular authorities alternated between active and passive resistance to schooling for the masses and any systematic attempt to provide education. Many members of the ruling elites themselves saw no purpose in literacy. Among the most noted illiterates were important kings such as Charlemagne and William the Conquerer, both of whom were satisfied to leave all reading and writing tasks to their clerics. They were not, however, adverse to having members of their families and courts tutored. But not far beyond the court. Subjugation, it was widely believed, required certain handmaidens among whom ignorance and illiteracy loomed large.

Both the secular and religious rulers of medieval Europe bear much of the responsibility for the squalor and ignorance that were the defining characteristics of the bulk of the population and for the system that allowed it. However, there was also a combination of both subjective and objective conditions and circumstances that contributed to the situation. The majority of Europe's people lived as tenants in relatively small rural settlements and villages, eking out a precarious living from the land while providing various services and paying onerous taxes, usually in produce, to their usually absentee landlords. Notions of social mobility and improving the lot of the individual, inherited with birth, were virtually nonexistent. People were born, lived, and died within the confines of their villages and social class. For them education and literacy had no value and were not even part of their world perception. If there was a book around, it was the Bible read by a local priest; if there were records to maintain they were the responsibility of either an overseer representing the landlord, or of the priest. There were neither books nor newspapers available to anyone. Literacy was not required or particularly valued, and clearly not pursued. If a child was chosen for schooling—a rare occurrence—it was under the aegis of the Church, and usually for the purpose of pursuing a lifetime in its service.

Books were not plentiful, partly because of the great difficulty involved in their production. Scribes—often monks—laboriously wrote out each copy by hand. Moreover, most books were written in Latin. All this made books inaccessible as well as expensive. Ownership was limited to the Church and to the very rich. There were relatively few titles, and few copies were available, even to those who could afford them. Newspapers were nonexistent.

There were, to be sure, pockets of scholarship and learning where reading was valued and avidly pursued. These tended to be in urban centers, often around the courts of various rulers, in and around the Church, and among some religious groups, most notably the Jews.

This was the situation regarding literacy in the Western world at the dawn of the fifteenth century as Europe began its emergence from what is appropriately labeled the Dark Ages. Over the next centuries a series of events occurred that transformed the predominantly oral culture of Europe into a written one, changing both attitudes and actual conditions dramatically.

The Renaissance

In the middle of the fifteenth century movable type was invented, apparently by different people in different parts of Europe more or less at the same time, although Johann Gutenberg is commonly credited with the invention. The printing press was to intellectual life in Europe what water is to a thirsty person. It seemed impossible to quench the thirst for new titles: within several years of the invention more books had been printed than had accumulated in manuscript form over the previous ten centuries. It also became possible to print and mass-circulate written matter other than books.

Perhaps the most significant short text printed and widely circulated was Martin Luther's *Ninety-Five Theses*. Luther nailed the original to a church door in the small German town of Wittenberg in 1517, thereby launching the Reformation. Uncirculated, the *Ninety-Five Theses* would probably have been regarded merely as a challenge to the Roman Catholic Church—which, indeed, they were—and dealt with internally. Widely circulated, they rapidly became much more, bringing a new, parallel, Christian dogma into being.

Among Luther's most significant teachings was that justification is by individual faith rather than by clerical mediation to God. This, of course, meant that all people should be enabled to read the Scriptures in their own languages. It was only logical, then, for Luther and other church reformers to urge the spread of literacy as a means of achieving personal knowledge of the Scriptures.

In the history of the spread of literacy in the West, the Reformation and the invention of print were the most significant events since the invention of writing. The two, functioning hand in glove, provided both the rationale and the means for an explosion in literacy and for the beginnings of universal schooling. Both encountered resistance. Books considered to be seditious and heretical were banned and burned. Protestantism was denounced and Protestant leaders were excommunicated and sometimes persecuted. But it was impossible to turn back the clock.

Europe's presses were responsible for a prodigious outpouring of printed matter of all sorts. People wishing to express themselves had the means to reach large audiences, and hence a new motivation to commit their thoughts to writing. And an increasingly literate public provided encouragement for both the writing and printing of material.

The spread of schooling, a natural consequence of these events, occurred rapidly. Protestants were generally in the forefront of this surge, with Catholics reluctantly following suit. By the mid-nineteenth century the notion of universal schooling had advanced to the point where the first compulsory education acts were passed. From then until the present the issues have centered on implementation rather than on the validity of education for all. Throughout the past four centuries emphasis on liberation and human rights has been coupled with a strong conviction that education and literacy ought to be universal and avidly pursued.

With the spread of literacy came a transformation in the perception of its value. Increasingly, literacy became more than a means for preserving the heritage of the past; it became a tool for the exchange of ideas, for debate, for invention and innovation. This evolution did not take place overnight. For a long period reading remained inexorably intertwined with religious texts, particularly the Bible, and had only extremely limited use in secular life. It was not required for job performance; reading was deemed necessary for moral rather than practical purposes. Readers were individuals, it was assumed, who had direct knowledge of the Scriptures and thereby were also possessed of moral fortitude.

While Protestant ministers were exhorting people to become literate, the Western world was becoming increasingly secularized—to be sure, only very gradually—and secular uses for literacy had yet to be defined. Slowly, during the course of the seventeenth and eighteenth centuries, there began to evolve the notion of an "educated man," or a "man of letters." It was historically premature to include women in this concept. The "man of letters" was an individual familiar with the literary and philosophical output of Western civilization—his familiarity gained, of course, through having read the classics as well as contemporary works. This was not an ideal that could be achieved by the masses—or even by the new bourgeoisie, whose members were frequently illiterate: it was at core elitist and appropriate mainly for an urban intelligentsia.

Urbanization

Beginning in the dusk of the eighteenth century and continuing throughout the nineteenth, a series of events occurred that had a profound impact on the spread of literacy. Despotic government and rigid class structure were subjected to challenge and revolution. The French Revolution, with its cry of "liberty, fraternity, and equality," heralded a new social order that swept through the West, giving new status and purpose to common folk, and giving birth to the middle class. Literacy very quickly became one of its hallmarks.

The Industrial Revolution soon followed, radically altering economic patterns, modes of production, and the rhythms of work, employment, and family life. It was attended by a massive movement of people that caused cities to swell and depleted rural agricultural hinterlands. Europe's population, with astonishing rapidity, was transformed from predominantly rural to overwhelmingly urban. Farming gave way to factory work; traditional rural patterns were exchanged for new city arrangements. Coupled with the new social climate formed by the earlier consolidation of the middle class, this emergence of a new urban working class dramatically increased the growth of schools and of literacy.

A schooled person was held by employers to be more desirable than one without schooling. Not atypical, for example, is the statement by one of the new industrialists, Alexander Calloway: "I have found from the mode of managing my business, by drawings and written descriptions, a man is not much use unless he can read and write; if a man applies for work and says he cannot read and write, he is asked no more questions."[3] Schooling and literacy were beginning to be valued for their potential contribution to the workplace and to work functions, albeit without any specific definition. Being literate was, to a large extent, still viewed as being something of a character reference.

Schools also served another purpose: they provided an institutional caretaking framework for children that made it possible for both parents to work—an economic necessity. While the motives for this aspect of schooling may not have been pure, one very important byproduct was that children were taught reading and writing.

By the middle of the nineteenth century the overall literacy rate in Europe was estimated to be between forty and forty-five percent, albeit with a wide spread: Sweden boasted ninety percent literacy while the Russian Empire, still largely rural, underindustrialized, and ruled by absolute czars, had at most ten. Fifty years later, at the turn of the century, schooling had become mandatory in most countries, employers were increasingly requiring school participation credentials as a prerequisite to employment, and literacy rates had surged to unprecedented levels. During those fifty years literacy made greater gains than in the previous nine centuries combined. Economic historian Carlo M. Cipolla, in analyzing these developments, remarked that "illiteracy was considered a national disgrace all over Europe, and as wealth increased a determined effort was made to devote more resources to the education of the people."[4] For literacy the nineteenth century was a watershed: it reversed prior attitudes and realities and heralded a new era.

There is one significant caveat to this picture: it is based on extremely flimsy data and is therefore heavily weighted by conjecture. Information about literacy before the twentieth century is derived from documents such as deeds, marriage registers, bills of sale, and wills—documents to which individuals had to affix their signature or mark. It is generally assumed by historians that a person capable of writing out his or her name was literate. By comparing the numbers of those capable of writing their names with population figures, literacy rates are computed. There is a controversy among scholars regarding this approach, stemming from a challenge to the assumption that name signing and literacy can be equated. It is quite possible that the rates cited are inflated. While literacy was clearly more widespread than ever before, it was probably at a very elementary level, and it is not at all clear what people were capable of reading or what they actually read. A large proportion of those counted as literate would be considered illiterate by today's standards.

Perhaps the greatest contribution of the nineteenth-century literacy explosion was the change it brought in perceptions of literacy and attitudes towards its inculcation. The position that literacy in the hands of the masses posed a potential danger and that, therefore, it should be restricted to certain ruling groups was firmly replaced with an ideal of a fully literate populace. The acquisition of schooling and literacy were henceforth deemed human rights to be avidly pursued. Governments were charged with—and generally accepted—that mandate.

The Twentieth Century

The past four score years have been critical in the further spread of literacy and development of new literacy concepts. World wars, technological advances, the attainment of independence by most of the Third World, the strengthening of democracies and the rise of new communist regimes, and a universal desire for economic growth have all, in their way, been contributory factors.

Modern Missionaries

In the immediate aftermath of the Russian Revolution the first of the modern literacy campaigns was launched by the new Soviet regime. Lenin, arguing that "an illiterate man is nonpolitical; first he must be taught how to read," placed this effort high on his agenda of national priorities.

At the same time, missionaries seeking to spread Christianity in the less-developed regions of the world also began placing increasing

21

attention on reading, which they viewed as an essential tool for gaining access to the Scriptures, and hence to conversion.

Ironically, these two activities were anchored in similar logic. For the Christian missionaries reading was the key to the "true religion"; for Lenin it was the key to the "new religion." Both coupled notions about reading with notions about the texts to be read—the Bible and the Communist Manifesto. Beyond that it does not appear that much attention was paid to the issue of the uses of literacy. In the best of early Protestant tradition, then, literacy continued to be viewed as a means for enabling individuals to become true believers and followers. Throughout the world, in numerous countries, both of these efforts have continued to the present, and have been responsible for raising literacy consciousness, if not for developing high levels of literacy.

The Modern Workplace

The most significant change, however, has grown out of a different agenda, one that has provided the very notion of literacy with new meaning. New concepts of the relevance of literacy to economic well-being have gained currency, for the first time seriously dealing with the function of reading.

In western countries workplaces became large, sophisticated, complex arenas no longer capable of sustaining themselves with word-of-mouth orientation and informal on-the-job training. It was found increasingly necessary to rely upon written materials as a central mode of communication and instruction. Written directions, manuals, descriptions of procedures—all of these made the workplace more reliant upon print than ever before. Mere literacy, defined in nineteenth-century terms as ability to sign one's name or recite the alphabet, was no longer adequate. Reading abilities had to be developed to levels that brought this new plethora of written matter within the purview of the people. Literacy itself became meaningful only when accompanied by a notation of standard or level, which in turn required definitions of functional literacy.

Once definitions were made—and, the process of definition continues unabated—the map of literacy attainment was altered. People who had qualified as literate were found to be functionally illiterate and in need of additional instruction. Primary school education, which in the past had been viewed as at least adequate to instill literacy skills, was found to be insufficient and in need of supplementation. Universal literacy had become a reality, but new definitions had transformed the old concepts of literacy into an anachronism. Further confounding this picture has been the furious development of alternative modes of communication, information storage and retrieval, and data processing, which—as Marshall McLuhan observed—might well render reading itself anachronistic. Even those who disagree with such radical assessments cannot ignore them.

The Third World

The emergence of the Third World has had a different but equally profound impact on twentieth-century literacy. Newly independent, impatient to develop economic infrastructures and activity, anxious to modernize, most countries in Africa, Asia, and Latin America regard literacy and schooling as necessary for achieving their goals. They accept without question the wisdom offered by the distinguished Swedish economist Gunnar Myrdal: "Obviously, advances in literacy and advances in economic development are interconnected."[5] A modern state, they reasoned, required a "modern" citizenry, and a central component of individual modernity was literacy. But what degree of literacy? Name signing and Bible reading may be of importance, but they contribute little to economic growth. Literacy had to be applicable to texts that would convey new ideas and techniques: ideas that could lead to change and techniques that could implement those ideas and accelerate the pace of change. Literacy, then, had to be developed at relatively high levels.

A dual strategy was adopted by most countries. One arm consisted of ambitious and costly plans to establish universal primary school systems that would assure the literacy—at least to the fourth-grade level—of all future generations. The other arm was based on the logic of Tanzania's President Julius Nyerere: "We must educate our adults. Our children will not have an impact on our economic development for five, ten, or even twenty years. The attitude of our adults, on the other hand will have an impact now."[6] Massive literacy campaigns were launched. A "quick fix" approach, these campaigns were intended to eradicate illiteracy with great rapidity. It was hoped that people with centuries-old traditions of illiteracy would be unable to "escape" becoming literate.

The strategy has been far from successful. To begin with, its logical underpinnings were flawed. Literacy is not just a technical ability: it is a consciousness that must be internalized before an individual can be available for instruction. In the absence of any cultural supports, "new" literacy wanes almost as soon as it waxes. This proved to be as true of reading instruction in primary schools as in adult literacy campaigns. Moreover, standards that were set were not realistically attainable. There were no texts available that had been specially written for new literates on practical matters. The introduction of change and development, it transpired, was not necessarily contingent on literacy, but on a host of far more complicated factors. Literacy was not the panacea; it was not even a useful palliative.

Results of the various efforts have not been surprising. Rapid return to original states of illiteracy seemed to be the norm rather than the exception. Dropout rates among people unaccustomed to classroom rhythm was inordinately high—often surpassing fifty percent. Teachers themselves were frequently only barely literate. Despite the strong motivation to attain universal literacy and the steps taken to achieve that goal, the results have been more than disappointing—they have in some ways been negative. There is a new generation that may despair of its ability to become literate—or worse, may have been confirmed in the notion that literacy is not the important skill that it was touted to be. At the very least, these efforts at rapidly spreading literacy have made it difficult to measure the state of reading in a given region: most of those who have attended schools or participated in literacy campaigns are listed by their governments as literate when in fact the overwhelming majority are not.

Despite the unhappy results, the Third World's literacy efforts have served, along with the industrial world's notion of functional literacy, to establish a new understanding of reading. Reading is now widely accepted as an attribute of a "modern person" and is understood to be a far more complex phenomenon than was previously realized. In addition, the concept of a "modern person," being among other things gender blind, has replaced the earlier concept of an "educated man." As the quest for universal literacy continues, more accurate definitions continue to evolve.

Literacy in America

America's first settlers—seventeenth-century adventurers, men of fortune, idealists, and refugees from Europe seeking to forge a new future—left countries in which printing presses were already churning out books in unprecedented numbers. Most of the settlers were already imbued with a strong literacy consciousness and actively sought to assure its perpetuation in the new colonies. Their motives were mainly religious. The Reverend John Cotton, in 1656, expressed a widely held view: "Learn them to read the Scriptures, and be conversant therein. Reading brings much benefit to little Children."

Literacy was deemed an important personal skill. Laws and regulations requiring the provision of schooling by local authorities, apprenticeship contracts stipulating that the teaching of reading, writing, and "ciphering" were among a master's obligation to his charges, court cases brought against offenders who had failed in this requirement—all bear ample testimony to the centrality of literacy in the world views of colonial leaders. Throughout the colonial period, records show, schools were generally found in those areas in which larger population concentrations made them viable: cities and towns. Children growing up in rural areas or in very small towns had little access to schooling. Even those who did attend seldom spent more than three years in school.

Colonial Times

Just how literate colonial America was is a matter for conjecture. Data derived from comparing signatures to marks on various documents suggest that the literacy rate among males was seventy percent on the eve of independence and had climbed to seventy-five percent by the end of the eighteenth century. Actual reading abilities were probably far less developed than these figures suggest. Historian Carl Kaestle estimates that approximately twenty percent of males were "sophisticated readers," meaning that they read books, newspapers, and almanacs. Historian Lawrence Cremin brings an important bit of information: Thomas Paine's *Common Sense* "sold a hundred thousand

25

copies within three months of its appearance and possibly as many as a half million in all. That means one-fifth of the colonial population bought it and a half or more probably read it or heard it read aloud."[7] If this was so then "real" literacy may have been somewhere between the level suggested by signatures and that estimated by Kaestle.

Leaders of the new republic continued to place a high premium on literacy. George Washington, for example, arranged for army chaplains to teach illiterate soldiers convalescing after the hard winter at Valley Forge how to read. Sixty years later, in 1838, Congress authorized the establishment of "post schools" to teach army recruits basic skills, stipulating that "the administrative council at each Army post [was] to hire a chaplain who would also act as schoolmaster." Although members of the clergy did not serve as teachers in regular schools as a rule, this congressional action was reflective of a widespread attitude that literacy was inexorably intertwined with the spiritual rather than the temporal domain.

Military Requirements

Throughout the history of the United States the military has played an important role in the spread of literacy. From its earliest days it was keenly aware of literacy levels among its recruits, maintained accurate records based on reading tests, and offered instruction to upgrade reading levels. It was the army that discovered, at the turn of the nineteenth century, that fully forty-two percent of its members were illiterate, then noted a century later that that figure had dropped to seven percent. In the twentieth century it was again the army that established the first minimum literacy requirement when it adopted a fourth-grade required standard for induction during the First World War, raised it to a fifth-grade equivalency during the Second, but then inexplicably retreated back to a fourth-grade requirement during the Korean War. All these determinations were based on some notion of functionality, albeit a rudimentary one.

The increases in literacy recorded by the army for the 1800s are largely a reflection of the spread of schooling. Like Europe, the United States was affected by the Industrial Revolution and rapidly expanded its school system. The rise of the "common school" was largely motivated by sincere notions regarding the significance of schooling, but also in part by a desire to provide conditions that would allow both husband and wife to work. Literacy had yet to be defined in functional terms; its main purpose was still religiously inspired. However, as schooling spread—and became compulsory in state after state—the ability to read, write, and "do" arithmetic increasingly became a prerequisite for employment, usually without employers being able to indicate specific uses for such skills. During the latter half of the century literacy became "secularized" and was deemed important for both labor-market participation and citizenship. As in Europe, literacy was also thought to be characteristic of a "lettered man," so much so that Webster defined literacy with the twin definition of "able to read and write" and "versed in literature and creative writing."

While espoused for all, literacy was not equally evident among all sectors of the population. Women did not lag far behind men. Rural folk and southerners fared less well than their northern compatriots; Black Americans had the lowest level of literacy. The ethnic and regional differences in literacy that persist to this day have early origins in the American experience.

Modern America

With the twentieth century some new themes were introduced. Waves of non-English-speaking immigrants arrived at America's shores and had to be "Americanized." That process, from the beginning, included becoming literate in English. The requirement of literacy for citizenship continues to be an important one; because of it, a multitude of newcomers has been motivated to learn the language and begin the process of absorption.

A second theme, already discussed, has been that of functional literacy, the idea that literacy is more than a matter of religiosity or general education but needs to be understood in relation to the function of the individuals within the society. Efforts to define literacy according to its function began during the First World War and have been growing apace ever since.

The third theme is more recent. With the growing awareness of rates of functional illiteracy among disadvantaged groups in the population—Blacks, native Americans, Hispanics, and the economically deprived—literacy instruction began to be viewed as an instrument of social policy. Literacy instruction, it was argued, would contribute to improving the social conditions of members of these groups. As in the Third World, literacy came to be regarded almost as a panacea.

The United States has always had a deep commitment to literacy. Definitions have changed, as have notions of precisely who ought to be literate. It would be misleading to condemn conditions and events of one era on the basis of concepts and realities of another. It would be equally wrong and misleading to gloss over present realities by treating them with the standards of the past.

3

Literacy and Illiteracy in the United States Today: A Question of Values

Inordinately high rates of illiteracy in America—almost at developing-country levels—have been claimed by a number of surveys conducted over the past ten years. Their findings become automatic and immediate headline-grabbers. Most recently a basic literacy test administered by the U.S. Bureau of the Census (1986) revealed that thirteen percent of Americans above the age of twenty are illiterate. *Time, Newsweek, U.S. News and World Report*, and all major national newspapers carried the "story" prominently. Robert Barnes, the Department of Education official who announced the results, noting that "it was a pretty simple test," calculated that between seventeen and twenty-one million adults are, in fact, functionally illiterate. "An abomination," railed Jonathan Kozol, author of a book entitled *Illiterate America*. On a national television show he claimed that the actual figure is substantially higher: sixty million. And there are others who have calculated that the correct number of illiterate American adults is higher yet: seventy-two million.

By contrast, a forthcoming study carried out by the prestigious Educational Testing Service places the proportion of unlettered at about four percent, and a 1979 Bureau of the Census study stated that only one half of one percent of Americans above the age of fourteen can be labeled illiterate. The concerned public is justifiably confounded. The figure is either very high or very low, a cause for either national worry or pride. What is, indeed, the state of illiteracy in America today?

The Definitional Dilemma

Unfortunately, the answer to that question is highly complex and devoid of drama—the truth is that all the figures widely quoted are correct and incorrect at the same time. While they all make use of the terms *literacy* and *illiteracy*, they differ significantly in the definitions they give them. If one uses a definition that appears to have been acceptable during the eighteenth century—the ability to sign one's name—illiteracy is negligible. If ability to read *The New York Times* is the criterion, even the high estimates are probably too low. If name signing is the bottom rung of the literacy ladder and ability to read treatises is the top, the "real" literacy level should be sought somewhere in between. But where?

During the past few decades scholars and educators have been conducting a search for such a benchmark—that level of reading ability that expresses the fundamental requirements of adult roles and functions, and beneath which people would be functional illiterates in modern American society. Once identified, it is assumed, such a benchmark would make it possible to determine literacy conditions with greater accuracy and to develop instructional programs with clear objectives.

The Search for Clarity

Two main approaches have been followed in the quest for the magic benchmark. One, used extensively by the military, has collected materials that are required reading in many military occupations and has analyzed them accordingly to various readability formulas. Results are expressed in the form of school grade level equivalencies. The desired standard is usually discovered to be somewhere between the eighth- and tenth-grade levels.

Another approach, employed by the Bureau of the Census and by the University of Texas in its well-publicized study in the early 1970s, eschews grade level definitions and creates "objective" tests that include a series of reading tasks felt by the researchers to be essential for adults living in the United States at the present. The recent (1986) Bureau of the Census test consisted of twenty-six such questions; the University of Texas study identified sixty-five objectives considered necessary for adult life and produced batteries of exercises to examine proficiency in dealing with them. These assignments included reading job advertisements, filling out job application forms, and addressing an envelope. Results were expressed in percentages, i.e., what percent of those taking the test were inadequate—and hence, functionally illiterate—for each task that was tested. Using different criteria, it is not surprising that the two studies arrived at dramatically different figures: the Bureau of the Census claiming that the functionally illiterate adult population numbers between seventeen and twenty-one million, and the University of Texas placing the figure between twenty-three and fifty-seven million, depending on the reading tasks thought necessary. This enormous disparity also serves as a fitting comment on the reliability of literacy statistics in general.

Both of these approaches seek to determine what functional literacy should be. The more traditional manner of measuring illiteracy is far more simplistic. Since 1840, literacy rates have been reported every decade on the basis of census figures. These, in the main, are derived from school attendance data: those who have attended school—first any school, and in later census reports those who have completed either four or five years—are deemed literate. The Bureau of the Census accepts the fourth- and fifth-grade designations of the military as appropriate benchmarks for the entire population and assumes that anyone who has completed that many years of schooling is therefore literate. Very low literacy figures, such as those claimed by the 1979 census report, are, then, actually measures of attendance and not of reading and writing abilities.

Not until the 1950s did the notion gain currency that people who left school after fourth or fifth grade may be illiterate. It grew out of a series of studies that revealed that schooling and literacy do not necessarily correlate and, indeed, that schooling was not necessarily a good predictor of reading skills. The Bureau of the Census, however, has yet to examine actual literacy abilities in the census itself and continues to report school-leaving data as an indication of literacy. Its 1986 study was carried out on a small national sample of 3400 people and did not emanate from a national census.

Literacy and Diversity

The basic premise that there is a definable functional literacy standard that has validity "from sea to shining sea" warrants examination. Technical literacy—the ability to identify letters of the alphabet and associate them with their sounds—is a skill that lends itself to universal definition. People either know the alphabet or they don't. In that respect, the terms *literate* and *illiterate* have constant meaning. However, functional literacy is far more complex and requires certain judgments about vocabulary and certain assumptions about knowledge. These, in turn, are derived from a subjective analysis of the environment rather than from an objective assessment of mechanical skills—"a summation of value-laden opinions," according to Professor William Griffith.

There is a question whether a country as vast and diverse as the United States can adopt and sustain one universal definition of literacy. Many scenarios can be projected, each of which represents different literacy needs and would yield different standards and figures. One scenario might project a stage that is rural, with family members engaged in farming, its social and cultural life largely revolving around the local community; another setting would be the financial community of a large city, engaged in the complex social and cultural activity of the rich and the well-to-do. Yet another setting might be a small factory town with a population active in the labor forces of various factories and involved in a variety of local social networks. Each setting constitutes its own culture. In each, literacy may have different connotations, different uses, and different support systems. It would surely be appropriate to define and measure literacy within these multiple contexts rather than against an artificial national standard. The result, of course, would be several definitions of literacy, each applicable to a particular set of circumstances, rather than one nationally applied level.

Those who oppose this approach generally argue that literacy is a vital facilitator of mobility; people unable to read and write, they suggest, are barred from participation in many activities and have restricted access to the workplace. They maintain that if literacy at a certain level—say, the ninth-grade level—were universal, unemployment would disappear and people would become more politically active and would be able to partake more fully of social and cultural experiences. The language of the Adult Education Act (Public Law 91–230), through which the federal government's efforts in coping with illiteracy and basic education are mandated, provides a classic example of this attitude: its stated objective is to "enable all adults to acquire basic skills necessary to function in society" so as to "make available to adults the means to secure training that will enable them to become more employable, productive, and responsible citizens." Presumably, the absence of literacy at a given functional standard creates a gap with exclusionary consequences. Moreover, adoption of multiple literacy standards would introduce a form of class structure obnoxious to fundamental American precepts of equality.

These arguments attribute to literacy powers that it unfortunately does not have. Neither labor market participation nor "good citizenship" are necessarily contingent upon reading and writing abilities. If they were, and if estimates of an illiteracy rate in excess of fifteen percent of all adults are correct, then clearly a great many "illiterates" work and pay taxes. Employment patterns are a function of marketplace demand and economic conditions, not of the availability of a literate work force. Similarly, if "responsible citizenship" is manifest, among other attributes, in the payment of taxes, these are levied on income: the Internal Revenue Service has yet to reject monies from the unlettered and certainly doesn't accept a plea of illiteracy as justification for nonpayment.

Literacy and Employment

Employers do not stipulate reading and writing skills as necessary job qualifications, according to the Department of Labor's *Dictionary of Occupational Titles* (DOT), which describes all known current occupations and lists the qualifications required to obtain them. Rather, they generally express educational requirements in terms of level of schooling completed. That some high school graduates might have difficulty reading and that some who didn't finish high school may read at advanced levels is a reality rarely related to. Labor market recruiters tend to place greater value on certificates and degrees than on specific abilities and substantive knowledge. Insofar as gaining access to work is concerned, it appears that certification is more significant than literacy. Only later, when people are actually working, do gaps in knowledge and missing skills come to light, and then only if they are actually needed for job performance.

A study conducted by the Center for Public Resources in 1983, *Basic Skills in the U.S. Workforce*, reported, "For the most part, companies responding to the CPR survey indicated that reading skills of out-of-high-school employees met or exceeded specific job needs." It appears from this study—unfortunately, one of the very few of this kind that have been undertaken—that reading deficiencies are not as severe as present figures regarding functional illiteracy suggest. To be sure, employers participating in the study cited instances of basic skill deficiencies, but these tended to be in areas such as writing, mathematics, reasoning, speaking, and science, not reading. Deficiencies identified were job specific; that is they were only identifiable in those job categories in which such skills were actually required. The fact that reading was not fingered suggests that it is either not required for most positions or that most people are able to handle job-related reading tasks.

Job retention is a function of performance and, at times, seniority. The linkages between reading and employment are far more tenuous than some of the literacy rhetoric would have us believe. Other basic skills form a different issue. They certainly ought to be included in notions of literacy, but when that is done, the literacy problem becomes more than merely one of reading skills. The figures widely touted as expressions of the country's literacy status purport to focus on reading rather than on a broader range of skills.

There are, of course, the unemployed: in recent years between seven and eight percent of the labor force. They are not, by any means, all illiterate, although those with lesser amounts of formal schooling tend to be overrepresented. Clearly, if there is unemployment the likelihood that the unschooled will be affected is high. Unemployment itself, however, is caused by economic conditions, not by educational gaps. If all people were college graduates capable of reading at very high levels, but economic conditions were such that full employment could not be sustained, there would still be unemployment. Many highly educated people were unemployed during the Great Depression.

A further issue often related to literacy is that of job mobility. Those unable to read and write adequately, it is argued, are hampered in their ability to move either up the employment ladder or laterally to other jobs. Again, literacy is only a relatively minor cause of the phenomenon. Movement occurs as the shape of the labor force changes, not as people attain greater reading skills. It is not possible for there to be only one level—at the top—with all people bunched there together. Even if everyone was highly literate, there would have to be a hierarchy, with some people at the top, some in the middle, and others at the bottom. Most workplaces depend on hierarchical structures. Lateral movement, too, is dictated by economic exigencies, not by levels of education of the work force.

It is frequently argued that individuals are affected by their low-level reading abilities because they cannot compete effectively with those with higher-level skills. Consequently, improved literacy is necessary to increase one's competitive edge. Reality, once again, mitigates the importance of literacy. After entering the labor force—which, as was suggested, relates more to levels of schooling completed than to literacy—a combination of factors affect advancement and promotion decisions. These include seniority, personal characteristics, interpersonal relations, and various performance criteria, among which literacy abilities do play a role, but only when they are really necessary.

Literacy and Citizenship

"Good citizenship" is cited as another outcome of literacy. However, "good citizenship" itself is only defined in the most general of terms. One aspect of citizenship behavior, widely accepted, is that of participation in voting. There was a period in history—reversed only in recent times—when illiteracy disqualified one from voting in some states. That measure, however, was not intended to disenfranchise illiterates but to deny the vote to Blacks. Therefore, if all Blacks in those states where this exclusion was practiced were found to be literate, it is fair to assume that some other exclusionary measure would have been found in its stead. If voting is an indication of good citizenship, there is no evidence that illiterates don't vote while their reading compatriots do. There is ample indication that there are a great many, both literate and illiterate, who do not exercise all rights and responsibilities of citizenship, particularly if the standard is set at voting at presidential elections. In the 1984 election only 53.3 percent of those eligible voted. To be sure, those with less than complete high school educations were underpresented among voters, although they certainly were not the only ones not to cast a ballot: 47.7 percent of those with eight grades or less of schooling, 46.7 percent of those not completing high school, 37.1 percent of high school graduates, 30 percent of those not completing college, and 20.6 percent of all college graduates saw fit not to vote. Greater amounts of formal schooling and, presumably, of literacy, correlate with voting behavior, but it would be incorrect to suggest—as some have—that illiteracy causes disenfranchisement.

Knowledge of events and awareness of public issues is, perhaps, another aspect of "good citizenship." Prior to radio and television, newspapers were significant channels of information. Today, electronic media are responsible for keeping people abreast of events without requiring them to read. At least a portion of the approximately thirty weekly hours that A. C. Nielsen estimates are spent on average by adults viewing television might be devoted to newsgathering. Literate or not, people can be fully aware of issues. Presumably, other criteria determine whether or not they choose to participate. And again, the specific role of literacy remains unclear.

The Dynamic Quality of Literacy

The purpose of these observations is not to denigrate the importance of literacy but to place it in perspective. There simply is no magical point of literacy at which individuals become employable, perform well in their jobs, carry out the responsibilities of citizenship, qualify for citizenship rights, or become good parents. It is therefore spurious to suggest that such a standard exists. Different definitions are needed for different situations; literacy requirements and literacy levels in the United States cannot be determined by a universal national standard.

This approach does not mitigate against egalitarianism, mobility, or competitiveness, even though on the surface it might appear to do so. Literacy skills are not static. Individuals do not achieve levels of reading ability that then become "locked in place" and cannot change. Instead, there is a dynamic quality to literacy; reading abilities can improve, but they can also deteriorate. There is evidence that lack of use results in loss of skills. Two recent studies, one by the Library of Congress and the other by the American Enterprise Institute, reveal that a high number of Americans don't read even though they presumably can, a phenomenon known as aliteracy. It is quite plausible that many such individuals suffer skill loss and are found to be effectively illiterate when tested, even though at one time they were perfectly able to read at acceptable levels.

The rise and fall of literacy skills can be understood within the context of demand. Assume that while in school people learn the mechanics of reading and continue to develop their abilities in response to the growth of their interests and the demands of curricula. While they are in school, their reading abilities rise to meet the demands placed upon them. There are, to be sure, those who somehow manage to sail through their school years navigating a course that succeeds in avoiding learning. This may be due to their own ingenuity, inappropriate curricula, the incompetence of teachers, or any combination of these factors. Most, however, carry out assignments and do develop their abilities and knowledge. Once they leave school—with or without a diploma—there are those whose life course leads in directions where reading requirements are limited or virtually nonexistent. Unless they are motivated to read on their own, such people are likely to become nonreaders. Several years later many will have lapsed into functional illiteracy. For the most part such individuals retain the fundamentals of reading; they know the alphabet and can associate the letters with sounds. When, at some later turn in life, they again find themselves in an environment in which reading is necessary, they are able to regain their skills and even improve upon them. This syndrome is not unique to literacy: virtually all skills developed during the years of formal education are subject to erosion in consequence of lack of usage.

Schooling has traditionally been regarded as a preparatory phase of life during which individuals are provided the knowledge and skills necessary for future adulthood. Nearly twenty-two percent of all adolescents leave school without completing high school, an additional forty-five percent choose not to continue their studies after graduating, and the remainder go on to various levels of further education. The amount of formal education obtained has a deciding influence on the nature of employment secured at the point of entry to the labor market.

Literacy in the Workplace

Employers generally follow the logic that more years of schooling translate into better preparation for the workplace. This logic, however, breaks down soon after employment commences for employees at all levels and with all manner of prior education and training. In the public and private sector, it has been found that however much preparatory education was received, people still require additional education and training to enable them to function properly in their jobs. Over the past few decades employers have developed training and education mechanisms of their own. It has been estimated that employer-sponsored education is almost as large, in monetary terms, as all primary, secondary, and higher education combined. Economist Anthony Carnevale has calculated that while the tab for all forms of formal education combined reached $238 billion in 1985, employers spent a staggering $210 billion on employee training and education. Virtually unnoticed, a shadow system of education has developed for adults after completion of the formal, theoretically preparatory, educational cycle. It certainly raises a big question mark around the concept of schooling as preparation for adult life and serves as a potent reminder that the process of education is a lifelong one. "Training outside the workplace does not create jobs," states Carnevale. "Jobs create training."[1]

Several surveys conducted over the past several years on the educational endeavors of the workplace have inadvertently shed additional light on the issue of literacy. While a few employers provide their employees with instruction in reading and writing skills—conventional literacy programs—a much larger number offer courses and programs carrying different titles that are, in fact, efforts to improve literacy. From courses in letter and report writing for corporate executives (sometimes called "executive communication"), through courses that seek to develop specialized vocabularies, to classes in expression, listening, speaking, and reasoning, the American workplace is constantly striving to improve the literacy abilities of its work force. Most of these efforts avoid the use of the term *literacy*, and those addressed by them are hardly thought of, or perceive themselves, as illiterate. However, it appears that there is a major and concerted effort to upgrade various aspects of literacy.

If an individual is found wanting in some job-related reading and writing tasks and requires specialized instruction to further develop these capabilities, such a person is functionally illiterate within that particular context, although he or she may be quite literate in another environment.

Literacy and functional literacy are relative terms that can only be properly defined in relation to specific contexts. As people move from situation to situation, or features of their patterns of living and working change, new conditions make it necessary to redefine literacy and literacy levels. Mechanisms—both formal and informal—usually come into being aimed at aiding people to attain the new standards. This is still another reason that there cannot be one universal definition of literacy that is suitable for all Americans, in all places, at all times. One can only agree with the verdict pronounced by psychologists Sylvia Scribner and Michael Cole following a study of illiteracy among the Vai people of Liberia: "While attempts to arrive at some overall measures of literacy competencies may be useful for certain comparative purposes, the representation of literacy as a fixed inventory of skills that can be assessed outside of their contexts of application has little utility for educational policies."[2] Such efforts have equally little validity for understanding the state of illiteracy in any one country, and certainly not one as vast and diverse as the United States.

Profiling Illiteracy

Since it is so difficult to arrive at an accepted and viable national definition of literacy, it is extremely difficult to estimate the scope of the problem. To do so accurately requires a mapping procedure that would identify the various environments around the country along with the actual reading needs in each, and then assess the abilities of those living and functioning within them. Thus far, however, most efforts have concentrated on painting national portraits of both need and incidence—a form of abstract expressionism.

Available data are such that one can draw only very general conclusions. Three sets of data need to be considered: school-completion information, readability studies, and specific national surveys of adult functional illiteracy.

School-Completion Data

The most important information to be examined in profiling illiteracy consists of school-completion data, not so much because of what they convey regarding actual skills and knowledge, but because of the importance given to such information in the workplace. People who drop out of school are in a position of relative disadvantage. They have fewer employment options, and once employed, they receive lower income, at least initially. Nationwide, thirty-six percent of the adult population has not completed high school. It is significant that lower levels of school completion are found in areas where employment opportunities are extremely limited and where occupations require little or no formal education. States that attract large numbers of immigrants are also likely to have low education levels. It is not surprising, therefore, to find a regional clustering pattern: dropout rates in southern states are the highest (half the population), closely followed by large immigration-drawing states such as Texas, New York, New Jersey, and Florida.

Historically, literacy and school participation have been highest in urban centers, with rural areas being at the opposite pole. The patterns of change are interesting: as industry has moved into rural areas, a new incentive has been created for school attendance and participation curves have begun a gradual upward swing. This can be seen, for example, in some areas of the South, where school attendance has been increasing over the past decade. Large cities, particularly those that are also ports of entry, are experiencing a downward trend brought about partially by immigration, partially by internal migration of opportunity seekers from areas in which unemployment is high, partially by the clustering of disadvantaged groups in the inner city, and partially by the flight of labor-intensive industries to more attractive areas.

There is no doubt that the less schooling people have, the more likely they are to be functionally illiterate. All the surveys agree on this point, even though they differ substantially in their assessments of the overall rate of illiteracy. The recent (1986) Bureau of the Census study, for example, found that fully seventy percent of those classified as illiterate had not completed high school. Similarly, the University of Texas study found the lowest levels of achievement among people who had left school.

Just what proportion of high school graduates is functionally illiterate is not known. Most, of course, are not, but many are. One indication of this can be found among students in community colleges, all graduates of high schools. Over half of community college entrants, researcher John Roueche found, are lacking in adequate basic skills: "The most offered courses in American community colleges were remedial reading, remedial writing, and remedial arithmetic."[3] His portrayal of community colleges gives rise to doubts regarding their ability to alter the situation: "Putting it bluntly, reading and writing assignments of any consequence or depth were rarely made in regular courses. Many of the students never purchased the required textbook or lab manual for a particular course or program because they had correctly discovered that reading and comprehending those materials were not necessary for successful course completion."[4]

Community colleges do not have a monopoly on remedial reading courses for high school graduates: a number of Ivy League colleges also make such courses available to entering freshmen who are found to need them. Evidently, many high school graduates cannot read at appreciable levels, and their inabilities are not always significantly corrected when they receive additional formal education.

Thirty states have declared that graduates of the twelfth-grade must be able to exhibit reading capabilities of at least eighth-grade level. In other words, in any situation requiring a standard of literacy at the ninth-grade equivalent or higher, many people with high school diplomas are functionally illiterate. Information about high school completion can provide only very broad notions regarding the current status of illiteracy.

At the point of entry into the labor force, high school dropouts are not likely to be hired into jobs that require much actual reading. Those with twelve or more years of schooling, however, might find it necessary to read on their jobs. As a result, those with less formal schooling will, in all probability, have fewer job-related incentives to read—or to acquire or improve their reading skills—than those with high school diplomas.

Noncompletion of high school is only one attribute of a very large group of disadvantaged people within modern society. Low income, abject poverty, inadequate housing, work instability, family instability, and membership in a minority group—especially Black and Hispanic—are other frequent attributes. Illiteracy is neither the cause nor the result of such conditions, but merely one of their manifestations. Illiteracy is almost always part of an intertwined web of circumstances. Consequently, literacy cannot serve as the cure for a cycle of disadvantage that afflicts an all too large segment of the population.

This does not mean that functional illiteracy is confined to the disadvantaged, nor is it a profile of those who do not complete secondary schooling, many of whom are not disadvantaged. However, it certainly does suggest that many people are likely to be illiterate because illiteracy, unfortunately, is part of a "package" of impoverishing attributes. It is not unreasonable to argue that if the cycle of poverty were to be broken through a concerted social and economic policy, literacy too would improve, almost as a byproduct. Literacy alone is not a panacea, nor even a palliative.

Readability Studies
Readability formulas to assess illiteracy require that actual texts necessary for functioning in specific contexts by assembled and examined. Since there have been very few attempts to do this, national estimates are based on a small number of localized and relatively specific studies. As a result, aggregated data are entirely unreliable.

The military has been at the forefront of this approach to literacy assessment, and has identified reading-level requirements ranging from eighth- to twelfth-grade equivalents, depending on the occupation being addressed. Materials such as newspapers, forms that people need to fill out, street signs, and public notices have also been periodically analyzed with similar results: the selection of standards between the eighth- and twelfth-grade reading levels as determinations of functional literacy. A number of ifs are involved: if the required standards identified are indeed those that form essential requirements of adult functioning, if performance of the various tasks for which the materials have been produced actually requires that they be read, and if the estimated proportions of those reading below the suggested grade levels are even close to accurate, then the number of adult functional illiterates may be somewhere between twenty and thirty million people. There are, of course, too many ifs to make this anything more than an educated guess.

If the readability approach were applied in all contexts, it could provide a precise picture of the state of literacy in the United States. However, available information is such that one cannot even make a rough estimate. At the present time, on the basis of the few surveys that have been conducted, it is possible to attach adjectives to the situation, but not figures.

National Surveys

Rectification of this sorry state of information cannot, unfortunately, be found in the few national surveys of adult illiteracy that have been made, even in the two most significant ones—those conducted by the University of Texas and by the Bureau of the Census. Neither, of course, was really objective. Both tested ability to perform tasks that were assumed to indicate literacy levels but around which there is hardly a consensus. In their effort to establish national conditions, both studies neglected regional and environmental attributes that might well suggest the need for other criteria. The U.S. Bureau of the Census might believe that thirteen percent of all adults above the age of twenty are functionally illiterate and the University of Texas may feel that its estimate of between twenty-three and fifty-seven million functionally illiterate adults is accurate, but neither figure can be confirmed, and it is not at all clear what they mean. Their main purpose, it seems, has been to throw a spotlight on a matter that has been identified as a serious problem without adequate elaboration or data. Most of the estimates that are bandied about are based on these studies and not on new, original research.

An Alternative Approach

Illiteracy is situational; it can only be defined in context and can only be tackled in context. An alternative to the national approach, then, would be to locate problems where they exist. While such an approach would render it impossible to state a national figure for illiteracy, it is not clear what the value of such a figure is to begin with. There is nothing particularly useful in the statement that one region ranks below another in its literacy rates, especially if the regions compared are very different.

Literacy assessments are valid only within the contexts in which they are made. They are closely linked to vocabulary, knowledge, and background. As these conditions change, definitions of literacy have to be appropriately modified. Account must be taken of literacy's perpetual dynamism.

Reading is more than a "functional" skill: it has value beyond its function as a vocational tool. It is intrinsically valuable as a means of self-fulfillment and continuous self-enrichment. Values such as literacy are built into culture, forming part of a larger mosaic. In an environment in which reading is not regarded as a value, it is unlikely that literacy will develop appreciably. To get to the root of the literacy dilemma, then, it is necessary to examine cultures. If a culture or subculture relegates reading to its periphery—or accords it no place at all—the issue is not one of individual illiteracy but of cultural illiteracy. The issue is different, its definitions are different, and the mechanisms for coping with it will necessarily be different.

In the United States today there are groups of people living in communities that place little if any value on literacy. They have evolved other means of managing the tasks that have been traditionally linked with reading. While members of such groups are possibly illiterate, the central issue is one of cultural illiteracy, which is built into cultural rather than individuals. In the search for national illiteracy figures this aspect of the issue has been neglected. The clustering of illiteracy in certain areas strongly suggests that there are illiterate communities—

groups of people living in environments in which literacy plays only a marginal role and where its acquisition is neither encouraged nor supported.

So long as such communities exist, illiteracy rates will continue to soar, no matter how many national literacy campaigns are waged. It is more than a question of teaching people to read—it is a question of reexamining values—community by community.

The general alarm regarding illiteracy in America results from the high figures that are given wide circulation. A population of twenty million adult illiterates is, indeed, cause for great concern. If the country harbors as many as sixty or seventy million illiterates, as some suggest, there is a national disaster at hand.

There is no doubt that manifestations of illiteracy, functional illiteracy, and aliteracy are widespread. For all the reasons given, however, it is virtually impossible to attach a responsible figure to these phenomena. Some definite trends can, in summation, be noted. The incidence of all three forms of illiteracy is highest among those with less than a complete high school education, among members of ethnic minority groups, in regions of the country with high unemployment, and among the economically disadvantaged. In all of these cases illiteracy is but one defining characteristic, interacting with other manifestations of disadvantage. It is absolutely wrong to jump to a conclusion that all minority members, or all of those not completing high school, or unemployed, or incarcerated are illiterate. Similarly, it is incorrect to assume that all high school graduates, all of the employed, and all members of the middle class are adequately literate. It is, unfortunately, correct to assert that illiteracy in its various forms is more likely to occur among the disadvantaged than among the advantaged. Indeed it does, at a ratio of two to one.

Illiteracy and aliteracy do not recognize socioeconomic boundaries. Consequently, these issues should not be viewed as affecting solely the disadvantaged. They are far more widespread, assuming different shapes and definitions as they move from group to group.

4

The Contexts of Literacy and Reading: Blaming the Schools

Individuals do not develop in a vacuum. They do not learn skills, accumulate knowledge, and form their ideas about what is important in isolation; they do so as members of a family, as students in a school, as players on a team, as workers, as watchers, as listeners, as citizens. Literacy, consequently, cannot be understood solely as an individual trait; it is also a manifestation of people's surroundings. Personal literacy and reading activity can most likely be found in those environments that support it; illiteracy and refusal to read will abound in environments where they are considered acceptable. To understand the problem of illiteracy it is necessary to consider some of the environmental forces that shape people's attitudes and behavior.

Schools

Blaming the schools has become a national pastime. When race relations become strained, the schools are blamed for not being integrated. When productivity shows slippage, the schools are blamed for not instilling the work ethic. When the nation falls behind in the space race, the schools are blamed for not stressing science education. And when reading skills are found to be deficient among large numbers of people, once again the schools are blamed.

At the same time, when budgets have to be trimmed, the schools are the first in line for cuts. The inadequacy of teacher salaries has long been identified as a major cause of school failure.

Schools, on their part, appear to be gluttons for punishment.

They readily accept any challenge given to them, giving the impression that they are capable of solving virtually any problem. Environment and the ecology capture public attention—schools develop curricula on the issue. Teenage pregnancies reach alarming proportions—schools dash in with "solutions." Drug use increases—schools develop "drug abuse" programs. Schools are a convenient (and relatively inexpensive) panacea. Such reliance is a confirmation of the central position schools feel they ought to occupy in society—and don't.

The Role of the Schools

Schools theoretically exist in a symbiotic relationship with the society they se·ve. To a large extent they mirror the society's prevailing attitudes and expectations. While they may be looked upon as agents of change, they are in fact severely constrained by the very conditions in which change is demanded. How can schools be effective agents of integration in a community in which parents are opposed to it? How can schools instill the work ethic in a community where there is no work? How can schools imbue their charges with positive attitudes towards the environment when adult members of the community abuse it? How can schools inculcate literacy and promote reading in a community where nobody reads?

These questions point to a central issue in education today: the extent to which schools can be expected to achieve objectives that are not supported by the community. Do schools, at best, mirror reality, or are they capable of transforming it?

Approaches to Reading

The teaching of reading has generally been approached by educators in a detached, surgical manner, with attention largely focused on curriculum and teaching methods. Which method of instruction, researchers have asked, is the most desirable—synthetic or analytic, phonics or "look-say"? Which readers are more suited to whom? Professor Jeanne Chall of Harvard University has summarized this quest for The Method in her classic *Learning to Read: The Great Debate*. Although much ink has flowed on the subject since its initial publication in 1967, the issues remain the same. Indeed, they are the same issues that concerned Tolstoy when he was a principal of a school in Czarist Russia. There seems to be a perpetual swing between the two basic approaches, although the cadence is not necessarily regular.

Since reading is an activity anchored in cultural variables, it is logical to assume that those variables will have an influence on methods of instruction. Before passing judgment on the efficiency of the techniques used, it is appropriate to place them in context.

Parental and community attitudes toward schools tend to fluctuate between two poles. On the one extreme are communities that have determined with a fair degree of specificity what schools ought to be teaching and how they should be carrying out their mission. Characterized by ongoing parental involvement, such communities encourage schools, interact intensively with them, support their accomplishments, and provide censure when such is deemed necessary. They are supportive communities.

On the other extreme are communities that regard schools as vaguely "important" institutions. Their importance may lie in their child-care function or in their offer of "book learning"—generally thought to be a "good" commodity. Just what should be taught and how are matters that are left in the hands of the "professionals." It is of course regarded as incumbent upon those professionals to provide whatever supports, encouragements, rewards, and punishments are deemed necessary—usually without external intervention. While such communities will support school *attendance*, they will remain uninvolved in substance and are consequently classified as *nonsupportive communities*.

Schools can perform best in a supportive community. They cannot, for instance, produce literate graduates against a backdrop of a nonliterate environment. They will experience extreme difficulty in graduating avid readers into communities of nonreaders.

School and Community

One question that often arises is whether schools can act to change a nonsupportive environment. Surely, the argument favoring such an approach goes, by producing a new generation of literate people, they can break the cycle of illiteracy. Unfortunately, the matter is far more complex. When schools seek to achieve something alien to the community, the effect of instruction is unlikely to be as dramatic as some might hope. Over several generations some advances may be made, but the likelihood of immediate effect is slight when the school lacks community support.

Communities

Everybody is a member of several communities: the nuclear family, the extended family, the neighborhood, the school, the church, synagogue, or other religious group, the workplace, the community center, social clubs, circles of friends. Each such community has requirements—stated or unstated—for active membership.

Modern communities differ substantially from their traditional predecessors. Communities of the past formed the environment into which people were born, in which they lived out their lives, and in which they died and were buried. Only rarely did individuals leave their communities of origin to seek their fortunes elsewhere. Mobility is one of the characteristics of the modern age. Traditional communities were all-encompassing social frameworks. They provided guidelines regarding childrearing, education, occupation, and marriage. They determined what one must know—and what one shouldn't know. They rewarded "appropriate" behavior and punished deviance. Where literacy was deemed desirable, it existed; where it was not, it rarely developed.

In the modern era, community influence functions in much the same fashion, but in a far more complex manner. Since individuals belong to several communities at the same time, they are subject to several sets of influences. However, even though there is a pattern of multiple memberships, the influences are usually interconnected. While there is an impressive **degree** of mobility across groups, most movement is lateral rather than horizontal. A member of a working-class family, for example, will usually associate with other working-class people, even though they may not be his or her neighbors. What this means in regard to values is that one usually associates with people whose values are similar, no matter how many communities one is a part of. Insofar as attitudes towards literacy are concerned, those who put no value on it seldom mingle with those who do.

Literacy is among those attributes that communities either endorse or ignore. There are few if any communities in the United States that display open hostility toward those able to read, but there are many communities that attach no importance to it. In such communities literate individuals are neither welcomed nor censured for their literacy. It is rather unlikely, however, that literacy skills can endure under such conditions.

There are probably many such nonsupportive communities spread across the United States. Schools functioning within them find it extremely difficult to overcome the apathy of the students and seldom achieve impressive breakthroughs. Adults members of such communities are not likely to seek reading instruction.

The spread of literacy requires the development of "literacy consciousness"—a task far more difficult than the simple teaching of reading and writing.

Families

Opinions are divided regarding the status of the contemporary nuclear family, some claiming that it is moribund—if not already dead—and others insisting that it is here to stay. Pessimists notwithstanding, the consensus seems to be that the nuclear family as a social institution is very much intact, although its functions have undergone major transformations over the past two centuries.

The ability of families to function with full freedom is somewhat limited by laws mandating participation in certain institutions. Compulsory education laws, for example, leave no room for families to decide whether or not schooling is necessary. But while laws can force families to send their children to school, they cannot force them to view schooling as an essential activity. Some families may not consider school to be of importance. Others might think of school attendance as important—maybe only because it is compulsory or because of its correlation with obtaining work—but may not have supportive attitudes towards what is learned in school. Children in such families will not receive the reinforcement necessary for succeeding in their schoolwork.

While families seldom engage in the formal teaching of reading and writing, they set the stage for its development—or nondevelopment. Children who are read to at an early age and who are surrounded by printed matter and reading activity at home grow up with an appreciation of literacy and an urge to become literate themselves.

Children who have no experience of reading and writing and who do not see older family members engaging in reading activities are deprived of role models for literacy. Approval by significant family members is a necessary facet of learning, especially in the early years. Schools cannot become substitutes for families: the prevailing attitude in the home helps determine what will be retained and what will be dismissed as valueless.

Family reinforcement is both formal and informal. An active interest on the part of parents in what has been accomplished in school constitutes formal reinforcement. Books, newspapers, and magazines in an active reading environment serve as informal reinforcement.

Nonreading families usually live in nonreading communities. It is not surprising, therefore, that illiteracy is found to exist among groups and is not usually a phenomenon that occurs in isolation.

Because individual family members have multiple associations, it is possible for a family in a nonreading community to be "invaded" by literacy consciousness—in other words, a person in a nonreading family may become a reader. When that occurs, several reactions are possible: the "invaded" family may change its attitude toward literacy—obviously the most desirable possibility—and begin an evolutionary process that ultimately affects all its members; the family, without changing itself, may continue to accept the reader as a member, a situation that has little if any effect on a community but could have a profound effect on a family; or finally, the newly active reader may find difficulty in reconciling the new behavior with the patterns endorsed by the family, creating a situation in which a choice has to be made and either the reading or the family has to be abandoned.

Families, then, play a key role in the acquisition of reading—a role so profound that no strategy for the spread of literacy can ignore it. In this regard, it is important to note that children are largely influenced by patterns they can see, not by those they are told about. Claims by parents that when they were at the age of the child they were avid readers, for example, have little impact if the child never sees them reading.

It is a common assumption that schooling can alter ingrained family patterns through teaching subjects unfamiliar to older families members—for example, that the learning of reading by a child will motivate the child's illiterate parents to learn to read. While there may be instances in which this pattern does occur, they are the exception rather than the rule. Similarly, it is unlikely that adult family members will learn to read because of shame or because of a desire to read to their young children. The more common pattern is, unfortunately, just the opposite: the attitudes of the older generation dictate those of the younger. Children raised in homes in which there is little or no reading become the next generation of nonreaders.

Families and the communities in which they function are not, of course, isolated from the larger society, one that places—at least in its rhetoric—a high premium on literacy. Why, one might ask, are communities and families not influenced by pro-reading attitudes? The answer is, presumably, that reading is not seen to be an activity relied upon for either information gathering or for recreation. Nor, evidently, does it play an important role in workplace functions. Rhetoric aside, people find it difficult to accept the publicly proclaimed attitude towards literacy and to see it as a desired—and rewarded skill. Slogans favoring literacy attainment do not change reading behavior. Explicit actions rather than unsubstantiated verbiage create the examples that children—and adults—follow.

A 1986 report issued by the U.S. Department of Education entitled *What Works* emphasize that reading to children is an important part of the process of teaching them to read. "Parents are their children's first and most influential teachers," the report states. "The best way for parents to help their children become better readers is to read to them—even when they are very young."[1] The report neglects to discuss how nonreading adults or illiterate adults can offer this help to their children. Clearly, the teaching of reading skills to adults is one component of achieving an increase in literacy. Far more important, and far more complex, is the process of instilling *reading consciousness* among groups of people who lack it. So much emphasis has been placed upon the functional aspects of reading that adults who do not require reading skills in order to function cannot believe the pronouncements they hear. For many adults, reading is just one of those things that schoolchildren have to do. Children, however, can only be serious about reading if the adults around them provide

53

genuine support and set real examples. Families, then, ought to be a prime target of those concerned with the spread of literacy. Without the active participation of families it is unlikely that literacy will become universal or that reading will become a more popular activity.

The Workplace

The overwhelming majority of adults enter the workplace soon after completion of their formal schooling. Since the workplace is the arena in which most daytime hours are spent, it cannot fail to have a significant impact on attitudes. As noted earlier, the workplace is also a major purveyor of education and training. Its influence on literacy warrants close examination.

At the point of entry into the labor market, records of educational attainment are usually examined. They are utilized by employers to eliminate those deemed undesirable in the workplace and to select those deemed capable of carrying out job tasks. The *Dictionary of Occupational Titles* (DOT), published from time to time by the Department of Labor, provides both a description of all current occupations and a listing of the qualifications necessary to obtain them. It is significant that successive editions of the DOT show fewer changes in job descriptions than in the required qualifications: the supply of candidates with higher levels of formal schooling has so increased that employers have raised the ante for jobs. Supply has influenced demand. An example of supply influencing demand in the opposite direction occurred when the army modified its reading-level requirement downward from the Second World War to the Korean War. Surely there was no parallel lowering of the tasks. In the immediate aftermath of the Vietnam War, with the introduction of the all-volunteer army, it was found necessary to recruit people with fairly low educational levels and train them in basic skills. Since that time the profiles of candidates have improved, enabling the military to raise entry level qualifications. It is the laws of supply and demand that determine labor market entry, not an objective, ongoing analysis of actual job requirements.

The labor market, through its recruitment practices broadcasts a clear message: certain levels of formal schooling are an absolute necessity if one wishes to gain access to jobs. The parallel message, relating to actual substance and skills, remains muted. Knowing company hiring policies, youngsters pursue diplomas, with little concern for the acquisition of actual skills and knowledge. To be sure, most people attending schools do learn something; the design of school curricula is not determined exclusively by labor market concerns. However, since diplomas constitute passports to the labor market, they are naturally emphasized. Obtaining certification of some sort has become a rite of passage from adolescence to adulthood.

In the workplace itself—once the hurdle of gaining employment has been surmounted—a different logic takes over. The performance of a job requires that certain functions be carried out. These, in turn, require certain skills and knowledge. It is at this point that the discrepancy between education and functioning becomes apparent. Employers have long recognized that entry-level abilities of employees need augmentation and have provided on-the-job training. When deemed necessary, they have even taught literacy skills, although training is usually focused on job-specific functions.

Apprenticeship has been an educational approach of the workplace throughout history. Early in the nineteenth century formal factory schools were established, growing into a large, unofficial, and uncoordinated system of education by the end of the century. Military training for conscripts has been practiced by armies for as long as they have been in existence. Regardless of new employees' education, job-related training largely takes place on the job and is imparted by employers. Having completed their quest for the formal qualifications that provided access to jobs, now employees need to obtain the skills, knowledge, and abilities that the jobs themselves mandate.

Literacy skills, during most of this century, have largely been considered to be among the entry-level abilities that new employees bring with them and have been only minimally dealt with within the workplace. To be sure, there have been important exceptions. Military branches have conducted literacy programs for nearly two hundred years. The early factory schools usually included a literacy component. More recently, a number of large corporations have begun offering literacy courses to employees requiring them, as have public institutions such as hospitals, universities, and some government units. Many labor unions have developed large educational programs for their membership. Such activities have always related to literacy at relatively low levels. They have sought either to impart reading and writing skills at very elementary levels, or to elevate existing skills to a standard thought to constitute functional literacy. Participants in such programs have almost always been at the bottom of the occupational ladder.

In recent years an important change has occurred, often overlooked in discussions of literacy because different labels are used. As needs have changed, so have real definitions of literacy. However, as those found to be deficient in abilities have been found further up the ladder, and as the skills and abilities that are focused upon become more sophisticated and advanced, the familiar—and value-laden—term *literacy* has been discarded. Many of the programs sponsored by employers can be found under titles such as "Executive Communication," "Corporate Writing," and "Listening and Reasoning." The object of all of these efforts is to develop existing skills to new levels in order to improve job performance. Over the past several decades there has emerged what one commentator has called a "shadow system of education," which has evolved new definitions of literacy and set about inculcating new "literacies" through a plethora of courses and programs. Unfortunately, workplace education in general, especially this aspect of it, is unresearched. Investigation into this vast arena of educational practice promises to reveal new and highly significant insights into both the definition and the spread of literacy.

Occupational moves—either lateral or horizontal—are usually accompanied by further training. Workplace educational networks place special emphasis on training for promotion, and such training often requires the learning of new skills. For example, a transfer to a new job might require learning a new vocabulary without which the written materials necessary in the new position are rendered unintelligible. Although not usually thought of as literacy programs, such programs qualify as literacy development.

Since skills often develop best in the context in which they are actually put to use, the workplace plays a significant role in the development of literacy, often unwittingly. A question arises as to the impact of workplace education on families and communities, and through them on schools. This remains an unresearched area about which nothing definitive can be stated. One might assume that the benefits gained by one member of a family from a company training program might inspire the younger members of the family with a new respect for learning and a desire to acquire literacy skills. It is likely, however, that many fail to draw the logical conclusions and that the transfer of attitudes from one environment to another is quite limited. What occurs in the workplace, seems to be regarded as limited to the workplace, with only minimal relevance for the family and the community. This is clearly an area that requires more investigation.

One possible hazard in these new developments is that, as workplace training becomes more sought after, less emphasis may be placed upon traditional education. People might begin concluding that the learning of certain skills can be postponed until such a time as an employer deems it necessary to impart them. There is some value in viewing school years as preparation for life, even if that preparation serves only as a basis for later training. The concept of education as a lifelong process, linked closely to workplace functions, could have the deleterious effect of turning education into simply the acquisition of certain skills. This, too, requires further research.

Technology

Since World War Two, television has assumed a growing—indeed, a central—importance in most people's lives. Studies reveal that children between the ages of six and eighteen spend more time watching television (18,000 hours) than they do sitting in classrooms (15,000 hours). Adults increasingly rely upon television for both information and entertainment. The electronic media, with television and its variations in the forefront, have rapidly become a major force in Western society.

The connection between increased television viewing and decreased reading has often been noted but has yet to be studied. While it is probable that time that might otherwise be devoted to reading is now spent in viewing, it is also possible that television has provided a new outlet for those who would never be readers, leaving the readers as active as ever. What is abundantly clear is that television offers an attractive and increasingly variegated alternative. Surrounded by such audiovisual riches, future generations of potential readers could easily be transformed into viewers.

Television and radio have become major vehicles for the dissemination of information. In *The Gutenberg Galaxy* Marshall McLuhan pointed out that print is no longer the major medium of communications. Whether or not this pronouncement is correct, it is certainly the case that a great many people depend on television for information. Not only does television present news events, it does so with an immediacy and vividness that cannot be matched by written news reporting. Are the electronic media replacing the more cumbersome—and less timely—conventional purveyors of the written word as the major service of information? There are no hard data, but several hypotheses suggest themselves.

The most optimistic suggestion, insofar as literacy is concerned, is that the electronic media have made it possible for more people to be informed in regard to a much broader range of issues than ever before. Those who in an earlier era would not have been readers at all—and would probably have lived without much information and with much misinformation—now have at their fingertips an effective tool for acquiring information continuously. Those who are readers can use the same tool to greatly increase the scope and efficiency of their quest for knowledge. Television broadcasts offer a constant flow of information both formally and informally. By simply viewing a program, people "pick up" information, whether it is sought or not. Certain "soaps," for example, are often cited as an important source of information on matters pertaining to health and medical care. It has been argued by some that nonreaders who were previously barred from participation in certain processes, such as the political, now have a mechanism that enables them to participate. For readers—according to this hypothesis—modern media are an Aladdin's lamp. Far more materials are being produced than ever before and are far more easily accessible.

Another hypothesis—pessimistic regarding literacy—is that television viewing is replacing reading. People who might have read in a former age now rely upon the electronic media for a combination of entertainment and information: television can offer classics more vividly than books; newscasts, commentaries, and documentaries replace newspapers, magazines, and journals; synthesized voice can blare out instructions, rendering manuals obsolete. What literary skills were for the industrial age, electronic skills will be for the postindustrial.

In between these two polar suggestions are any number of possible variations. In the absence of good data, it is only possible to hazard a guess as to the actual impact of modern technology on literacy. My own attitude is biased towards reading. The general broadening of horizons made possible by television will itself lead to a quest for literacy. Professor Ray McDermott of Columbia University's Teachers College has noted that the question is not whether people can acquire literacy, but whether literacy can acquire people. The electronic media aid in the latter process, I would argue, in a manner that has no precedent.

One important attribute of electronic media—television in particular—is their pervasiveness. Most homes have at least one television set, and a rapidly increasing number have access to wider programming through video recorders, cable television, and satellite receivers. People are enabled, through this medium, to extend their geographical, social, and cultural boundaries to encompass the whole world. Nuclear families are no longer isolated and self-sustaining as in the past. Through the little box in the living room people are increasingly able to become members of a global community.

Television could play a very important role in the spread of literacy. It could imbue people with the notion that literacy is a vital aspect of modern life. Does it perform this function? Few studies have been made, but a few days of viewing the most popular programs reveal very little, if any, conscious attempt to portray reading activity.

Imagine an individual living in an environment in which reading is considered a marginal activity. Reclining in front of a television set and tuning in to most programs will only serve to reinforce that view. The heroes and heroines who represent a desired form of living are seldom shown reading, and if they are, the activity is of only secondary importance. What people see on television for the most part represents what they want to attain. Literacy is not portrayed as a significant vehicle for attaining it. This is a lost opportunity; it acts to reinforce nonreadership.

The BBC attempted to spread a literacy consciousness in Great Britain through a television blitz several years ago. Numerous spots were aired, extolling the virtues of literacy and informing the illiterate how they might acquire this all-important skill. A similar effort is being made in the United States. But the literacy spots are given negative reinforcement by the programming that surrounds them.

Television is a potent force in shaping attitudes. Viewing may be a passive activity, but broadcasting is inordinately active.

In this chapter several environments have been examined. Each, it is contended, has an impact on its members, guiding them in the formulation of their attitudes towards a wide range of skills and knowledge, among which are literacy skills.

Although schools play a part in the development of literacy, as do individual abilities and personal preferences, the individual's attitude toward reading is not formed independently of the various environments through which he or she moves.

The causes of illiteracy, then, is not the "failure" of the schools. The question of who is to blame is a far more complex matter, reflecting the dynamics of interlocking frameworks, among which families, communities, workplaces, and the media play key roles.

5
Literacy and Learning

There are twenty-six letters in the English alphabet. Just how difficult can it be to learn them, to memorize the sounds that each symbolizes, and to put them together to form words and sentences? Many nonreaders learn skills far more complicated. Why, then, has the acquisition of reading skills, seemingly so simple, been so evasive? There is, unfortunately, no easy answer.

The dilemma of effective reading instruction has spawned a centuries-long quest for the perfect teaching method. New courses are continuously being published and hailed as "the answer" to the reading problem. Each new technology that becomes available is immediately pressed into service: television's contributions include the famed *Sesame Street*; computers are programmed to provide individual, self-paced courses; interactive video technology has turned its unique features to confront the issue. And yet, somehow, all the instructional tools and teaching programs available cannot successfully grapple with the task of teaching everyone to read.

The Department of Education has recently informed us that the answer lies in the teaching of phonics (relating discrete sounds to their letter symbols and then combining them into words): "Recent research indicates that, on the average, children who are taught phonics get off to a better start in learning to read than children who are not taught phonics."[1] Phonics approaches were pervasive until they were supplanted by the "whole word" or "look-say" method (identification of whole words followed by their analysis) during the 1940s. The pendulum has now swung back. Indeed, the pendulum of reading instruction methods has been in constant motion for generations. It is likely to remain moving in perpetuity. It is also possible that the problem does not lie in the methods used for teaching, but rather in the neglect of a proper analysis of how, why, and what people learn.

The Adult Learner

Adulthood is a stage in the life span achieved after the preparatory periods of childhood and youth; it is the stage in which special rights and responsibilities are assumed. In different societies, at diverse times, adulthood has begun at different chronological ages, depending on the life patterns that have prevailed. The late physicist and educator Professor Jerrold Zacharias once defined an adult as "anyone older than anyone else." Surely a sixteen-year-old appears to be adult to a six-year-old. However, in the present age a sixteen-year-old is considered an adolescent, still very much in preparation for adulthood. In earlier times sixteen-year-olds were considered adult, ready for marriage and parenthood. Biologically, the age at which individuals are transformed into adults is determined by puberty; culturally, the age may vary widely from one society to another.

The Age for Learning

The phase of life that precedes adulthood is a period of preparation for that which follows. Most societies mark the transition with "rites of passage." Confirmation and bar mitzvah, which at one time were rites of passage, are now regarded as being largely ceremonial events. Graduation from college, the acceptance of a career job, and getting married are the modern equivalents of rites of passage. "Today," the saying goes, "you are an adult."

The designation *adult* confers certain rights but also carries new responsibilities. Popular expressions underscore this notion of life-span development: accomplishments of children and youth are praised with phrases like "exhibited adult behavior" and "are no longer children." Old age is at times referred to as a second childhood, a reversion to childlike dependency, in recognition that many adult roles and responsibilities have been relinquished.

Theoretically, the preparatory phases—childhood and adolescence—constitute the training ground for adulthood. That is why the focus of education over the ages has been on children and youth;

adults have been virtually ignored. Consequently, "the archives for the study of adulthood still wait to be created," as Stephen Graubard noted in a 1976 issue of *Daedalus*. "Despite the growth of interest in the human life cycle," he commented, "we still know too little about the 'stages' of adult life, not nearly enough about the transition from adolescence to adulthood, and surprisingly little about middle age, let alone senescence."[2]

In other eras adulthood was a relatively static stage of life, but in our time the pace of change has accelerated. Adults experience constantly expanding horizons, changes in the workplace, changes in family life patterns, and changes in the world around them. Preparation that was deemed adequate in the past does not prepare one for sustained participation in the modern world; learning itself has become a vital coping mechanism. It would be spurious to suggest that adults in previous eras did not learn, but it would not be amiss to point out that contemporary adulthood relies upon constant new learning in an unparalleled fashion. Today's adults are forced to become lifelong learners just to keep abreast, and certainly in order to continue growing. The lines of demarcation between the preparatory and adult phases of life have become obscured, making it increasingly necessary to understand the process of adult learning.

Learning Deficits
Only in recent years have social and behavioral scientists begun devoting attention to the question of adult learning and the ways in which it differs from the learning processes of childhood and adolescence. Our present knowledge of the patterns of adult learning is wholly inadequate, still at an embryonic and tentative stage. An important breakthrough has been the widespread acceptance of the notion that learning can and does occur throughout the life span. While there are many different interpretations of this assumption, it has served to focus some necessary attention on the study of the adult as a learner.

One widely held notion has, as a result, increasingly come under attack. It was—and in places still is—held that the most significant learning had to occur during the childhood years because what was not learned at "the right time" could not be learned later. Deficits would begin to mount and would eventually become irreversible. Thus, for example, if literacy was not acquired by a certain age, illiteracy would become "fixed." One practical result of this notion has been the heavy emphasis accorded early childhood development programs. The earlier a person "begins," it was argued, the greater the chance of avoiding the accumulation of deficits. This theory is, of course, inimical to adult education: if deficits cannot be corrected during the adult years, or can be corrected only with great difficulty, those with learning deficits become a lost generation. Rather than provide such adults with educational programs, this approach would emphasize stepped-up efforts with their children.

Lifelong Learning

New theories, derived from empirical evidence, have strongly challenged the notions of deficit accumulation and irreversibility. According to these theories, learning can and does occur throughout the life span and that which wasn't learned at what educators once considered the "right moment" can be learned in adulthood; the "right moment" is determined by the adult's own ordering of events. It is not that adults cannot or do not learn, some new research suggests, but rather that the manner in which learning occurs is unique to each adult.

Conventional wisdom in regard to adult learning is perhaps best summarized in Benjamin Bloom's *Stability and Change in Human Characteristics:* "We do know that intelligence as it is presently measured does reach a virtual plateau in the period ages ten to seventeen and that further development is likely only if powerful forces in the environment encourage further growth and development."[3] In the absence of such "powerful forces," presumably, learning stops or at least diminishes. It is also probable, however, that the problem lies in the way intelligence is defined and measured and with the parallel that is often drawn between it and learning. Moreover, "powerful forces" do not have to be cataclysmic events: any change may be able to provide the impetus necessary to generate learning. The focus needs to be shifted from the artificial issue of whether adults learn to the far more useful question of what and how people continue to develop during the adult years.

Fusion of Past and Future

The fusion of past experiences with future aspirations determines learning in the present. This interaction is probably the central attribute of adult learning and clearly requires amplification.

From birth through adulthood individuals accumulate multiple experiences and are subject to myriad influences. Such experiences and influences combine to provide each individual with a definition of self, a clear picture of his or her expected actions, attitudes, roles, functions, and positions during the adult years. They provide the information necessary to perform in those roles, develop the requisite skills, and instruct succeeding generations in the appropriate attitudes.

Banking Education

In traditional societies early experiences had a virtually definitive impact: lifestyles generally followed those of the previous generation in predictable cadence; the functions for which people were prepared were those they subsequently carried out throughout their adult years and eventually passed on to their successors. Change was slow, often spanning several generations. New learning, as a result, was equally slow. Indeed, since adult life patterns were defined during the preparatory phase and then became a self-fulfilling prophecy, there was hardly any point in learning new things. When a person assumed adult status, that person's skills and knowledge were complete. Past experience dictated the nature of the future.

In the modern era this pattern—drawn here in broad strokes that obscure some of the detail that would explain the changes that did occur—has come undone. Adulthood is far more difficult to predict because it can change within any one life span many times and in many ways. Social mobility, geographic mobility, unplanned events that alter life patterns for large populations, technological advances—all have introduced an uncertainty that makes it virtually impossible to predict what a child will experience in adulthood. In no country is this more pronounced than in the United States, where mobility is a cultural hallmark: where one's past may be "interesting," but not confining; where—in theory at least—"anything is possible." This is a society that takes pride in the humble origins of many of its leaders and places heavy emphasis upon individual attainment. To be sure, in practice the idea is not always evident, but it remains a beacon of social philosophy.

This means that it is no longer possible to treat youngsters as if they were savings banks into which deposits of knowledge are made that will carry them through life. Modern education is more like a theater than like a bank. It is possible to set the stage and fill it with some props, but each person's life story will be played out in new and different circumstances. New lines have to be continuously learned, and the ending is never predictable.

The term *banking education,* suggested by the noted Brazilian educational philosopher Paulo Freire, is derogatory: Freire views the concept as confining and subjugating. "Banking" approaches to education are no longer practical because people and life spans have been liberated from the lock-stepped patterns of the past. Adulthood in contemporary society is fueled by new and constant learning.

Adult Motivation

Learning that takes place among adults is a process that must rectify past lessons with future aspirations. New realities have to be linked with the past, as the past is not easily shed.

According to conventional educational theory, motivation is a precondition to learning. Motivation, in this sense, is essentially a desire to achieve some change that cannot be accomplished without the acquisition of new skills or knowledge. Wanting change, people become available to learning that is viewed as necessary for reaching sought-after objectives. They remain unavailable, however, to learning that is not viewed as meeting that requirement. In this respect adults are selective learners: each individual determines his or her own goals, then charts a learning path, often subconsciously, directed at realizing that goal. This is not a one-time occurrence: it is a continuous, virtually lifelong process.

An adult who is resigned to his or her "fate," who believes that station and life pattern are not subject to change, is an unlikely candidate for new learning. Members of today's version of traditional static societies—may well feel that their life patterns are unalterable. It is in such groups that resistance to new learning is most likely to occur.

Conversely, an adult who believes that change is a constant possibility and strives to achieve it usually displays a willingness to learn and actively seek learning experiences. Adult learning theorist Allen H. Tough argues that most adults engage in self-motivated "learning projects" aimed at facilitating the changes they seek.[4] Such people believe that the way in which they define themselves and the way they are defined by others are inherently alterable. They also recognize that they have it in their own power to decide how this is to be done—and to do it.

There is yet a third category of individual, particularly pertinent in the American experience: the individual upon whom change has been thrust. New immigrants, for example, find themselves having to cope with a new culture, a new society, foreign ways. While some might seek to hold on to past behavior in their new surroundings, they eventually must conclude that the environment is more powerful and gradually, at times grudgingly, adopt new ways. This is a pattern quite typical of many immigrant groups. Upon arrival they established a pattern of life with which they were familiar—Chinatowns, Little Italys, Central and East European *Landsmanschaften*—small enclaves in which they sought to perpetuate that which they knew and with which they were familiar. Such creations almost always maintained languages of origin. Over time, however, it became apparent that compromises would have to be made in order to render survival possible. One very important adaptation was the adoption of English, first as a second language, which made communication with the larger outside community possible, and finally as a first language. Other immigrants have chosen to strive for integration—Americanization—as rapidly as possible, thereby supplanting the old with new. Change itself, however, is usually gradual, beginning with the adoption of outward manifestations of the new culture, such as dress and food. Deeper content follows, step by step. In both cases the changed circumstances have required the initiation of a learning process, reluctantly and slowly in one case, avidly and rapidly in the other. A vision of a future that differs from the past is in all instances a vital first ingredient in the adult learning process.

Ties to the Past

One very important part of every individual's "past" consists of ties to family, friends, and community. Severing such links is often an excruciating experience—one that most individuals try to avoid; the vision of the future that determines adult learning experiences is very often a group phenomenon rather than a purely individual one. Since change, however desirable, is difficult, people who are seeking change are apt to seek confirmation and support from a community of people from a similar background. Both goals and learning experiences assume communal attributes, whether or not the entire community shares in them. It is not uncommon, for example, for a family to decide that one of its members will walk a different path from the rest of the family in order to attain an objective—a future different from that which the family seems to be headed for. For instance, a family may decide to support a member who is preparing for a professional career or a career in the arts. Support can assume various forms, such as financial aid, reduction of time-consuming family responsibilities, creation of space, and active interest in the learner's accomplishments. The personal objective becomes a group objective and the entire group is galvanized to assist in its realization. In turn, the individual walking the unknown path reinforces the group decision and justifies its supports through his or her accomplishments, possibly paving the way for others to follow. Change, in this example, occurs not only for the individual, but ultimately for the entire group. There is individual learning and at the same time a group learning experience, so that in a very real sense the entire group is transformed. Such a pattern is more realistic than one that focuses attention on individual attainments that are not shared with one's community.

Adults do not live in a vacuum. Their lives are intricately interwoven with their environments, which in turn form central aspects of their "past." Change and learning, then, must also be viewed in a broader context of community. Pasts and futures are shared experiences.

Visions of the Future

Pasts that were devoid of literacy can be transformed into literate futures only if the visions of the desired future include literacy either as a means or as an end in itself. It is more usual to find people viewing literacy as a vehicle for change rather than as its main goal.

People become available for the acquisition of literacy only when their perceptions of future goals include reading. It is unfortunately rather easy for positive attitudes towards literacy to turn sour and become part of a negative past. Consider, for example, an individual who has arrived at the conclusion that reading skills must be acquired because they have been presented as a key to some future aspiration, say a new job. The learning task accomplished, the newly literate person applies for a job and fails to get it. For that person, literacy turned out not to be the vehicle for achieving the desired goal. This lesson becomes part of past experience, and when the next attempt is made to define objectives, literacy will in all likelihood not play a role. In the interim, of course, what literacy has been acquired may be lost.

In another scenario, the newly literate succeeds in obtaining the desired position, only to learn that literacy, after all, is not really required. The lesson incorporated into past experience would essentially be the same: literacy is superfluous and the efforts devoted to its acquisition unnecessary.

Such scenarios, while oversimplified, illustrate a process that makes the instilling of literacy a far more difficult job than many of the crusaders for the cause realize.

Reality of the Present
Dr. Cedric Beeby, formerly director of education for New Zealand, tells in *The Quality of Education in Developing Countries* of a meeting he had with tribal chiefs in Papua and New Guinea in which he sought to obtain their support for the creation of a system of schools. He suggested that the curriculum ought to relate to their needs and environments: be "relevant." The chiefs, who were quick to realize the importance of schooling for their future agendas, reminded Beeby that his own school experience had included instruction in Latin and Greek, insisting that it be a part of the schools he was about to establish. No amount of argument could sway them: their position on this matter was adamant. Latin and Greek, in the end, was offered in the curriculum. Schooling, in the perception of these chiefs who

themselves had no direct experience of it, was a "package deal," indivisible. Accepting its desirability, they insisted on the entire package and rejected what they probably saw as an attempt to market a watered-down version. It was the school as a structure that they accepted as being the bridge connecting past and future, not the substance that schools impart. An associate of Dr. Beeby's recently told me that several years later, after schools had functioned for a while, the chiefs were able to relate to specific content and were only too happy to part with instruction in the classical languages.

Literacy is perceived differently at different stages and in different contexts. An individual or community seeking change might view literacy as an essential component of that change, but literacy at that stage might be seen more as a form than a substance. An "educated person," it is assumed, has to be able "to read." Just what it is that one is supposed to read—and why—are matters only marginally considered, if at all. Later, after literacy has been acquired, its actual value and uses become evident. If the experience has not been as important as was originally envisioned, both the process and the skill may be discarded. If reading has begun to play an important role, it is reinforced and becomes available for further development.

It is not enough that people are motivated to acquire literacy or develop it to higher levels of ability. Literacy must assume a real role in people's lives if it is to endure. While the process of acquisition is a learning effort that occurs in the present, that "present" is a transient phase that derives its justification from the real contribution it makes to the future. Not only is the present temporary, as soon as it has passed it becomes part of the past where, firmly embedded, it will influence further efforts for change.

Availability for Learning

Adults are discriminating learners. Their learning mechanisms operate only in those areas where the adult has decided to apply them. An adult who is ready to learn is termed available for learning.

Being available for learning implies readiness to change in some aspect of one's life. A vision of a new future, whether clear or vague will generally determine the area of learning. Those areas in which people are comfortable—in which past experience and future aspiration mesh—are usually closed to new learning. It will always be the agenda of the learner and not of the teacher that will determine which areas are open to change and which are closed.

An illiterate person becomes available for literacy learning only when he or she perceives the need to develop literacy skills because they have become part of a goal that person wishes to attain. If a person does not perceive literacy as necessary, it is unlikely that there would be a favorable response to literacy instruction.

Effective instruction, of course, is that which leads to learning. It has commonly been assumed that effective instruction is a result of effective teaching. It is probably true that the method of instruction plays a role, but that role is a secondary one at most. It is the availability of people for learning that will ultimately determine whether or not instruction will be effective. This, then, requires that greater emphasis be placed upon identifying those areas where the student is available for learning. The search for the "perfect" instructional approach is futile. The focus in adult education has to be on *what* to teach—which is determined by areas of availability in the learners—and not on *how* to teach. Content selected by instructors because it is of importance to them will not necessarily seem important to the students.

Areas of Availability

One difficulty in this approach is to identify the areas of availability—that is, to discover what the students are ready to learn. There are several possible methods, all of which are based on the principle that in discussion with their peers people tend to focus on those areas of their life in which they would like to bring about change. These are "areas of dissonance," sources of discomfort that individuals are seeking to rectify.

Areas of *extreme* dissonance are not widely shared—such areas require therapeutic approaches. Even those available for discussion usually emerge only when the people are familiar and comfortable with each other; it is unlikely that dissonant areas will be discussed with strangers. By "tapping in" to discussions that are held among people of similar backgrounds who have come to know and trust each other, a great deal can be learned about developing programs that will meet their needs.

When the needs of the students are understood, instruction can be directed to those areas where learning will in fact occur. By directing instruction to members of a group, rather than to unrelated individuals, a group dynamic is created and becomes, in itself, an important aid to learning.

Several experiments have been made with this approach—albeit too few to provide a definite endorsement of the concept. However, in the experiments that have been made participation has been active, drop-out minimalized, learning has occurred, and subsequent retention has been high. This strategy, based on precepts of adult learning, offers an important and viable approach to the instruction of reading and writing to adults.

Implications for Literacy

One of the major problems in teaching literacy is that adults who come from environments where literacy is not valued do not see literacy as a necessary achievement. It simply plays no role in either past experiences or future aspirations. Such people are, according to this theory, unavailable for literacy instruction. If they attend programs at all, they tend to drop out in large numbers. Those who somehow remain will often relapse later into their original states of illiteracy. On the other hand, adults for whom literacy is an objective will be available for learning and will respond to instruction.

Because of the changing contexts in which people relate, availability for literacy is not a constant. A person who cannot learn to read at one period of his or her life may learn quite readily at a later period when literacy has come to be perceived as a desirable goal.

Literacy cannot be accomplished in one fell swoop, as many would prefer. But, by a complex process of identifying groups that are available for learning, the "teachable moments" can be found. Instruction might then prove effective.

Literacy itself cannot be forced upon people. A demand for its acquisition—on the part of the people to be taught—is a necessary precondition. Such demand is not born in a vacuum. It reflects people's social, cultural, and individual needs; it is intricately interwoven with the learners' past and their vision of the future; it occurs only when the learner feels an inner need for it; it is self-reinforcing; it is accepted only because that learner wants it, not because some other person says it is important; and it relates to time and space. Unless these conditions are met, literacy will not be acquired. Nothing is "good" because it is held to be so in the abstract. No abstraction can determine for all people what they will accept. Acceptance has to be personal. This, perhaps, helps explain the complexity of the literacy issue. As long as it remains a remote abstraction and is not seen as a concrete need by the individuals concerned, it cannot become universal, regardless of the effort and money spent on its behalf. Exhortations on its importance cannot convince people that it is either necessary or desirable. Slogans cannot define the future that individuals envision for themselves. Only the people themselves have that power.

Happily, the same analysis can provide a measure of comfort. A strategy based on the needs of people—as they themselves perceive them—can transform the vision of universal literacy into reality.

6
Lessons from Literacy Programs

NEW YORK: Over a ten-week period, forty-two men gathered three times a week in a downtown school to attend classes organized by their union. Divided into three groups, the men all received instruction preparing them for certification exams in their profession—bug and rodent extermination—mandated by the Environmental Protection Agency. Employees of New York City's municipal government, most of the men had been working for varied periods of time but had been unable to sit for or pass the examination: their literacy abilities were insufficient for reading the background manuals required for the exam—or for reading the questions on it. Several had a record of failed attempts with the test. For all, the certification conferred upon passing was a prerequisite for job security and permanence. Some of the men were native Spanish speakers, still uncertain of their facility with English. Asked to write their names and addresses, many scrawled large, shaky letters typical of children making their first efforts. However, all members of the group had basic reading skills, that is, they knew the letters of the alphabet and could make out words, albeit often laboriously.

The union sponsoring the activity originally believed that a conventional literacy program was necessary, feeling that improved reading abilities would provide the skills necessary to read the manuals upon which the examination was based. They agreed, however, to conduct an experiment in both curriculum and teaching methods largely because prior experience with conventional literacy programs had not been satisfactory.

In designing the curriculum, conventional reading development approaches were discarded. In their stead, it was decided to use the manuals themselves as basic instructional materials, even though most of the participants were unable to properly read them. These manuals, it was surmised, contained material with which the participants were familiar, which related directly to their work, and which would be of interest. By focusing attention on the substance rather than on the act of reading, the course would be transformed from a literacy program to a professional training workshop. Reading development, it was assumed would follow if participants became sufficiently involved in the subject matter. Since the men already had acquired elementary reading skills, the challenge was to develop these skills through application rather than through irrelevant reading exercises. Clearly, the central teaching approach had to be that of group discussion and not a structured read-in.

A second feature of the experiment was that actual teaching was performed by six members of the group, all exterminators themselves who had succeeded in passing the exam earlier. Each group was directed by two individuals working as a team. At first the participants, as well as the instructors (who were called tutors), were wary of the situation. It was unfamiliar and unconventional. How would the students be able to learn from their peers, in the absence of "real" teachers, and how would the tutors, never trained in "teaching," be able to carry out their mission? Perhaps more nervous than the men was the professional educator directing the course. She had agreed to participate in the experiment but found herself cast in a new and unfamiliar role—that of a coordinator and consultant to a group of tutors who, in theory, knew nothing about what they were supposed to be doing.

Fears were rapidly allayed. The participants and the tutors were both enjoying the experience immensely. Class discussions were animated and involved. None of the people felt as if they were pupils in a structured and uncomfortable environment. When one or another individual encountered difficulties in reading a text, help was quickly and usually informally provided, either by one of the tutors or by a classmate.

An outside observer may have had some difficulty in recognizing the proceedings in each of the group sessions as being classes. The activities were varied: small group huddles, conversations between tutors, conversations between a tutor and a participant, readings from the manual, discussions among all members of the group, formal authoritarian teaching, preparation of individual and small-group projects on matters pertaining to extermination, and just good fun.

The men were happy to be engaged in a professional seminar and were proud to share their participation with their families, who, in turn, were happy to provide encouragement and support. If the seminar had been presented as a course in literacy, they may well have regarded the experience as one they wanted to hide. They must have liked the experience, for they kept coming back, session after session. Not only was there no attrition, but by popular demand the course was extended for several weeks. Two important events occurred at the end: all the participants were able to pass their qualifying examination, and a large group asked for a continuation of the course so that they could achieve higher professional levels. There was yet another consequence. The tutors, so uncertain of themselves at the outset, felt increasingly comfortable as the weeks passed, and all asked to be able to continue as "faculty" in future endeavors. Further, in true union fashion, they formed a small group to press for better pay for themselves in their new role.

This experiment has some interesting lessons. First and perhaps most important, the substance of the program meshed with each participant's personal goals, in relation to both professional concerns and job security. Second, the program's literacy component was relegated to a secondary, nonthreatening position with which even the least literate in the group could cope. Nonetheless, it was ever present, and the goal of improving literacy skills was accomplished, virtually without pain. Third, members of the group were comfortable throughout, as they were surrounded by peers—including their instructors; they formed a natural support group. They also found support from their families and from the community as the seminar was viewed as a positive and worthwhile undertaking. Fourth, the men's own desire for change was the focal point of the course. It was not marginal to their lives but central.

SAN DIEGO: Twenty-five men and women are sitting in a class in a downtown adult learning center. They are all new immigrants from Vietnam, having arrived in the United States within the past six years.

Two of the group's most recent arrivals had roamed around South Asia for several years before finding the opportunity to emigrate. All live in an area of the city populated predominantly by Vietnamese. All but four have jobs. Most are married and the parents of children who are attending local schools.

Vietnamese, of course, is the preferred language of the group: it is also the language of the members' families and community. English—broken English—is spoken only while working and conducting business with outside institutions. Before and after class sessions animated conversations are held in Vietnamese.

The instructor is a young woman who has been a teacher of English as a second language (ESL) for the past three years. This is one of three classes she teaches, one in the mornings and two in the evenings. She has studied the teaching of English as a second language in a local university, enjoys her work—despite complaints regarding salary level—and has formed deep attachments to her students. She often visits their homes, where she is an honored and welcome guest. While she has picked up several words in Vietnamese, she does not know the language.

Lessons are structured, based on a series of textbooks which systematically and sequentially teach reading (using a phonics approach), introduce vocabulary words, and present short texts containing information or stories on various aspects of American life. The central object of the program is the teaching of English, including reading and writing skills, and its secondary aim is to assist participants in acculturating to their new environment.

Motivation to attend is high—at least initially. All the participants realize that knowledge of English is vital in the United States, and they are anxious to become part of their new society as rapidly as possible. This desire, however, is tempered by realism. Since most of them have been here for some years, the class sessions are not their first introduction to English. Most have managed to pick up a fair amount through their contacts at work and with various agencies and institutions. These experiences have taught them that English is not an easy language to learn, and most do not expect to achieve fluency by the end of the course—that accomplishment will occur, they hope, as their children, many born here, grow and develop. Their realistic expectation is that the course will improve their English language skills, help in the development of reading abilities, and contribute to their understanding of "how America works"—an area in which their experiences have been baffling. The course, they feel, will not affect their abilities to obtain better jobs or in any way help in improving their economic status.

They like coming to class. It gives them an opportunity to get together with friends on a regular basis, the instructor is popular, and the students can raise questions about various matters that arise from day to day. Unofficially, the class sessions have assumed an additional function as an information bureau.

As the months pass, the level of language ability of the students develops perceptibly, especially during the informal parts of the class, when information is shared or student daily life experiences are examined. There is a great deal of laughter during those moments.

Reading skills, however, seem unaffected by the proceedings. Students are reluctant to read, especially when asked to do so publicly in front of their classmates. They later inform the teacher that reading is the one activity that has no carryover or application "outside."

After a year the class is terminated. Participants hold a closing party, during which all events are conducted in English. The spoken level of English, although far from perfect or fluent, has certainly risen. Haltingly and shyly, two of the participants read short poems they have composed. Four months later, when classes resume at the learning center, eight members of the group enroll at a higher level. The others visit on occasion, although with decreasing frequency.

This ESL class is typical of many conducted around the country. It succeeds in sustaining student participation for several reasons: the members of the group are all of the same community, and the class has become, in a large sense, an "endorsed" community institution; the teacher is liked and flexible enough to depart from the written texts in order to devote a portion of each session to answering queries on issues of concern to group members; there is a sincere desire to acquire greater facility in English; and the participants have come to feel that attendance is helping them in the process of absorption into American life.

Although dropout has not occurred, those aspects of the curriculum in which participants have less of an interest are not effectively learned, particularly reading skills. None of the members are readers in their own language, although some are literate in it, and few have found that reading skills are helpful in either obtaining employment or advancing up the job ladder. Never part of past experience, reading is something they have submitted to because they believe that it may be important, but in this respect they have found the American experience no different from that which they knew before.

To a person, however, they understand the importance of schooling and are anxious that their children receive it. As for themselves, they are resigned to being part of a transitional generation. There is nostalgia for their past, an attempt to maintain important elements such as community, language, and foods. But there is an intense desire to become American, and they all feel that participating in ESL classes will help them do so.

CHICAGO: An adult basic education class has convened at a local community college facility for its eighth session. There are twelve people in the class—eight fewer than at the start of the course, only one month ago. Class sessions are held in the evening. Most of the participants are unemployed welfare recipients; three arrive directly after work. A mixed group, they all live around the general area of the college but belong to different communities: eight are Hispanic, three are Black, and one is white—a recent arrival from Kentucky. Although the course is labeled "one to three"—meaning that it is considered the equivalent of a first- to third-grade level—participants tend to have some reading abilities, albeit their levels are mixed. Although it is a year-long program, participants are required to re-register every eight weeks to satisfy the state funding source that enrollments have not declined. Dropout and turnover are high, with as many as half the faces changing every two to three months.

The curriculum is a mixed fare. A few textbooks are used for the teaching of reading and writing skills. Using a phonics method, the books present the letters of the alphabet, are heavily illustrated with objects intended to represent both letters and their sounds, and contain many exercises along the order of "Fill in the missing letter" or "Draw a line from the letter to the appropriate picture." In addition, much time is spent on the teaching of arithmetic, both from prepared sheets and from problems brought to class by students based on their own experiences. A minimum amount of time is spent on discussion, usually initiated by the teacher. The discussion is seldom lively.

The teacher is a professional adult educator, a thirty-year-old who has attended a series of training programs and has been certified as an adult basic education (ABE) instructor. She is in her fourth year of employment but retains a temporary status and, like all teachers in the program, is still paid—not well—on an hourly basis. She enjoys her work but is angered by her working conditions. While she likes her students and tries to develop closer ties with them, she is frustrated in this effort by the rapid movement of participants in and out of the course.

In the current class there are three participants who are attending their second year of the "one to three" course. Even though their attendance during the first year had been sporadic, they were "graduated." Nonetheless, they have reregistered. The teacher thinks this odd, but she has encountered similar situations before and has not bothered to question the three as to the cause of this repetition.

Progress is slow, almost imperceptible. The teacher tries new ways to engage her students: she searches for materials, often creating her own. She tries to talk with the students before and after class to determine what it is that they are looking for. But the pattern persists: attendance remains sporadic, dropout remains high, and it appears that progress is excruciatingly slow.

This class is typical of many ABE classes around the country. Their clientele, at the lower levels of prior ability, are largely composed of minority-group adults, many of whom are school dropouts. Even those who persevered somehow avoided learning most of the prescribed school curriculum. Their participation in ABE classes is an attempt to break the cycle of poverty and disadvantage in which they find themselves, but it is often a frustrated attempt.

Not knowing what to expect when they first enroll, they soon discover that the proceedings bear little relation to their lives. They are constantly subject to pressures that conflict with regular participation. Irregularity in attendance, they find, creates gaps that cannot be bridged. Their families and friends are generally not actively supportive of their participation: at best, they are passive; at worst, they stand in opposition. Since the group itself is usually heterogeneous, it cannot provide meaningful reinforcement. The result: people simply do not remain in classes very long. The actual dropout rate is probably higher than the reported rate of nearly fifty percent, as many classes report numbers of participants and do not indicate rollover (replacement in the rolls of one name by another when someone drops out and someone else joins the group).

Among ABE students there is one group that performs better than the others and exhibits greater durability. This group consists of people with higher ability and prior formal schooling who are motivated to attend as a precondition to taking courses that lead to a high school equivalency certificate (GED). This certificate is deemed important because it has labor market value. The bulk of ABE students, however, are caught in a web of disadvantage from which they cannot extricate themselves. ABE classes offer some hope, but unfortunately it rapidly evaporates.

WALL STREET: In a well-appointed room in the headquarters building of a large multinational corporation a group of six senior executives—managers and vice presidents convene for two hours each week over a two-month period. They do so on company time. Meeting with them is an instructor in writing, engaged as a consultant from one of the city's universities. The participating executives were only recently elevated to their present positions. All are college graduates; three have graduate degrees.

During each of the sessions the instructor introduces a different form of writing that an executive may be called on to produce, such as a letter, a memorandum, or a report. After presenting a few examples with the aid of a video tape, she gives the participants a writing assignment, tells them to whom it should be addressed, and briefly discusses with them its form and content. Writing exercises follow, and the results are discussed by the group. A series of expensively produced manuals that accompany the program contain detailed examples of different forms of address and text. The course is known in the company as "executive writing."

The participants in this course are all literate in the usual sense of the term. However, in their new posts they are required to write letters, reports, and memoranda with which they have not had prior experience. Soon after assumption of their new jobs they discovered—as did those to whom these documents were addressed—that they were having difficulties in formulating sentences, in using words correctly, and in making their point. This course is intended to assist them in all of these.

A growing number of employers in both the public and private sectors have responded to similar situations by developing courses of instruction aimed at improving the written expression abilities of their employees. These are not literacy programs in the conventional sense of the word, but they have attributes that qualify them as literacy activities. Their participants are individuals whose abilities in writing, and possibly in reading as well, have proven to be inadequate. Participants, aware that their skills require improvement, attend willingly and apply themselves to the learning tasks at hand. Clearly, their motivation to improve is high, and the changed circumstances provide the necessary impetus, as well as support, for learning. Moreover, none of the participants feels that they are in a literacy program: they are attending an executive training session—which has a wholly different connotation.

While there is some, mostly anecdotal, evidence regarding the effect of this type of program, it is unclear whether observed changes result from having attended or from having gained experience while actually performing on the job. Many of the curricula used in such activities are created "generically" by small private firms and marketed as "off-the-shelf" programs. Logic would dictate that the more remote the actual substance from the specific writing tasks that have to be engaged in, the less effective the actual program. However, some of these curricula may play an important role in increasing awareness of various writing problems—a precondition to their correction.

ST. LOUIS: Thursday afternoon. Margaret Smith, a volunteer literacy teacher, has arrived for her weekly session with Rose Baxter, a Black, single mother of three. The meetings between the two have been taking place over the past month. Mrs. Smith has attended a brief, two-day training session, during which she was instructed in the use of various materials and provided with some pointers regarding various aspects of her new avocation. She was assigned to Mrs. Baxter by the local organizer and meets with her at a learning center. The sessions last up to an hour and a half. Together, the two read materials that Mrs. Smith brings with her, write short messages, and spend some time on simple arithmetic calculations.

Progress is slow. While the meetings are pleasant, as time goes on less time is spent in formal learning and more in conversation. The two have forged a relationship that has become important to both, but it has become more of a "big sister" activity than a literacy class. Mrs. Smith has become increasingly frustrated by her seeming inability to teach her charge how to read. While Rose responds well to Margaret's efforts and appears to look forward to their meetings, she is making no discernible progress in her studies. Margaret has discussed the matter with her organizer, who counsels her to continue with her efforts but provides no clue as to how the situation might be corrected. Five months after beginning these sessions Margaret takes a vacation. She informs her organization that she will be visiting her own children for the next two months and will resume voluntary activities upon her return. As no other volunteer is available to fill in, Margaret asks Rose to return to the center at the end of the two-month period. Upon her return, Margaret tries to contact Rose, but Rose has moved and no one knows how to reach her.

Some seventy-five thousand individuals around the country are tutored by volunteers each year. In homes, learning centers, community halls, and prisons a small army of dedicated and well-intentioned volunteers devotes unremunerated time and energy to helping less fortunate compatriots. Not all experiences are like those of Margaret Smith and Rose Baxter, but neither is their story atypical. For as long as they last the contacts between tutor and tutored evidently fill mutual need and are important to both. They are, however, transient relationships, and their long-term effects are unclear. Different participants seem to derive different benefits from the experience. For some the caring is important, for others the contact with a representative of another community; some find the conversation helpful, and some are interested in improving their basic skills. Have beneficial objectives been met? In most cases, yes. Has literacy been improved? In most cases, no.

Volunteer-based efforts have often been advocated as the solution to illiteracy. There are many ways in which volunteers are used:

individual tutoring such as that described, instruction of larger groups in a more formal structure, recruitment of potential learners, assistance in child care while mothers attend classes. Volunteers perform important functions, but they are not "the solution." Illiteracy is a highly complex social issue that does not lend itself to a simple "cure."

PHOENIX: A local community college. Placement examinations given to the incoming class of students have revealed that almost half have difficulties in comprehending written texts and answering questions about them. Many exhibit limited capacities in mathematics. Those scoring under a certain level are assigned to remedial classes. The remedial sessions are highly structured, following a textbook distributed during the first session. Instructors are members of the college's English and mathematics departments, hired because they have attained graduate degrees in those fields. Most have doctorates, a few are completing their studies in the nearby university. None has been trained specifically in the teaching of remedial courses.

The students—who represent many different groups residing in the area—are variously motivated. Some are anxious to learn the material being presented so that they can pursue their studies. Others seem bored by the proceedings and invest only very limited energy in their classwork. The instructors do not mingle with the group. They teach carefully planned lessons, follow the textbook religiously, and periodically check their students' development through intermittent examinations. At the end of the semester about half the members of the class pass, some marginally, others with high grades. The remainder appears not to have advanced at all. Many enroll in other courses—including those who have failed. Some discontinue their studies altogether. Some will repeat the remedial course.

Community colleges everywhere can report similar experiences. An unfortunately high proportion of entrants—high school graduates—cannot read or write well enough for college-level study. During the first year, and often beyond, much of their time is devoted to remedial activities. Despite the major efforts made, the results are often disappointing. Survey after survey has pointed out the poor level of entry skills and underscored the difficulties in correcting them.

Can it be possible that so many young people simply cannot read well enough to attend college, despite special programs of instruction? Are the instructional methods inappropriate? Are the instructors inadequately prepared? Could the fault be in the materials being used? Possibly. But it is also possible, indeed probable, that there is no fault to be assigned. The skill levels that are encountered at entry to community college are a reflection of the environment in which the students live. They are an indication of the extent to which literacy is valued in that environment and of the extent to which individual members have been infected by the value of their community. The poor achievement records of the remedial courses are only partially a comment on the instructional methods. More significantly, they are indicative of the inability of the community college to instill in its students a sense of purpose that can override the attitudes instilled by the community. The community college experience is by definition a temporary one—a means to an end that exists in "the real world." That world, in turn, has defined its values clearly, and colleges have not convinced people of the need for redefinition.

If colleges are to be more successful, there has to be a neater "fit" between what they are seeking to accomplish and what the community appears to be demanding. Unless such a convergence exists, the college cannot in the full sense of the term be a community institution. This is particularly true of community colleges.

"Community college" is a label that implies belonging to the community. A community college cannot function merely as an alternative to regular four-year colleges. It must seek to anchor its curricula in the needs of the community it serves. By developing appropriate and relevant curricula, community colleges could have a greater influence on their students and could ultimately change attitudes towards literacy. So long as they merely reflect the community's attitudes without genuinely addressing themselves to the community's needs, they will be severely hampered in realizing their potential.

HARTFORD: The insurance capital of the world. Several of the large insurance companies have established elaborate training and education facilities here. One of these institutes occupies an ultramodern structure covering the better part of a city block. It is well equipped with lecture halls, classrooms, learning laboratories, a fully computerized resource center, television studios with satellite transmission capabilities, and a hotel to house out-of-town participants. As its brochures aptly state, everything about it is "state of the art."

Computers have revolutionized the insurance industry to such an extent that it is incumbent upon each of the companies to rapidly spread "computer literacy." The institution in question has established what amounts to a computer school, housed in a special wing of the facility. Courses of varying depth, complexity, and length are offered to all levels of the company's workforce. The courses are highly structured and quite intense. They cover aspects of computer use, from simple technical mastery of personal and micro computers to programming and maintenance of large main frames. Since the field of computers in general is advancing rapidly, courses—and, of course, equipment—must be constantly updated and participants exposed to several cycles of training.

At least at the outset, instruction in computer use must establish a common base of computer literacy, including a basic understanding of the computing process and knowledge of the specialized language that has developed. *Bits, bytes, RAM, prompt, memory, directory*, and *menu* all have highly specific meaning in a computer context and must be understood, indeed integrated into one's language, as a precondition to gaining mastery. The company sponsoring these courses has a strong interest in their success. So do the participants, who realize fully that computers will soon become fundamental work tools, if they haven't already. Any who harbor doubts in this regard rapidly learn that they are out of step with their work environment. Computer instruction at this corporate education and training institute is extremely effective.

Instruction in the use of computers has become commonplace. With unparalleled rapidity the computer revolution has swept through the workplace, the school, and the home. It has suddenly become necessary for large numbers of people to acquire literacy in a new medium, to learn a new vocabulary, and to learn new skills. The spread is not, by any means, universal. However, it is instructive to review some of its central attributes. Only a decade and a half ago computers were large, almost futuristic machines housed in special centers under special conditions. Computing was a profession deemed appropriate only for "the best and the brightest." Those without excellent mathematical skills, it was commonly held, "need not apply." But that has changed dramatically. Computers have become popular tools and been put within easy grasp of "regular" people. This popularization has had its influence on language and on our view of basic skills—it is increasingly considered essential for tomorrow's citizens to be masters of the computer.

An innovation that has taken root so solidly could do so only through a convergence of events and forces. The computer had to gain acceptance as part of the life pattern of the community. Its vocabulary had to become integral to the language. And above all, it had to garner the active support of individuals—people had to become willing to make changes in their own attitudes and behavior in order to acquire computer literacy. Surely there are lessons to be drawn from this experience in regard to reading and writing.

Around the country, in numerous settings, using a multitude of curricula and varied instructional approaches, catering to diverse groups with equally diverse requirements, are a great many literacy programs. Some are identified by that label; many are not. Some revel in their accomplishments; others bemoan their failures. Collectively their experience provides incontrovertible proof of only one point: there is no one correct way, no best way, to teach literacy. As people and the communities they live in change, as their past experiences and future aspirations diverge, so too must the educational programs designed to meet their requirements.

The assumption inherent in most literacy efforts is that literacy is "good" and that it is the same for all people. The experiences of literacy programs have raised questions about that assumption. People learn what they themselves define as "good." At different times and under changed conditions their definitions change. At all times, however, people will reject instruction that does not conform with their own perceptions. It is both superficial and artificial to adopt a policy that all people must attain a uniform minimal level of literacy skills.

Some literacy programs have been more effective than others. Some are able to sustain participation and generate learning; others experience high dropout rates. This does not mean that the seemingly better programs are superior, and it certainly does not mean that they are a panacea. It means only that some of the programs are appropriate and others are inappropriate.

An appropriate educational program is one that caters to a specific group of participants, deriving its content and methods from the group's needs. Such a program would seek to address topics that are meaningful and desirable for its participants and would focus on helping them to realize the objectives they have set for themselves. Once achieved, the initial goals will be supplanted by others. Since the learning process is an unending one, adult learning should not be considered in terms of single, discrete courses but rather as a lifelong undertaking that continually defines and redefines its objectives, always on the basis of the learners' needs.

Inappropriate programs are those that seek to impose agendas because their sponsors believe them to be "right," but which have no meaning for the participants. Such programs create boredom. Reaction quickly asserts itself through irregular attendance and attrition. There is, unfortunately, another possible reaction, less perceptible but far more severe. Uncomfortable and nonproductive educational experiences can confirm for some individuals that change is not attainable, that they must always live in the situation from which they have been trying to escape. By participating at all they are grasping for something, trying to accomplish something that, to them, is of value, only to be told—implicitly or explicitly—that they are reaching for the wrong thing. Intimidated, they may avoid future programs of instruction, not wanting to submit themselves to unnecessary discomfort and humiliation.

Appropriate educational activities can be of enormous benefit. Inappropriate ones at best are wasteful and ineffective. At their worst they are destructive and harmful.

There are appropriate adult literacy programs being conducted everywhere. There are also many that are wholly inappropriate. Several studies of adult literacy programs have been made, and they should by all means be studied. But the successful programs should not be blindly copied; they should serve only as a source of ideas that might be useful. By combining sensitivity to the needs of the learners, understanding of the process of adult learning, and knowledge of appropriate methods, programs can be vastly improved. The result will not be a uniform system of adult education, but a variety of activities that reflect the variety of American life.

7
Why Be Literate?

A case can be made for the position that literacy is desirable but not essential. It is increasingly clear that literacy skills can be supplanted. Oral directions can replace manuals. Television and radio can replace newspapers and recreational reading matter. Movies and tape recordings can replace books. Cameras can make written descriptions irrelevant. And how easy it is to use these technological wonders! Television and radio work with a turn of a knob, tape recorders with a flick of a switch, cameras with a snap of a shutter. A turn, a flick, a snap—and after that, eyes and ears take over, sifting through images and capturing sounds. No cumbersome alphabets, no lengthy periods of learning. And anyhow, the argument could continue, universal literacy has proven to be elusive after centuries of effort, while television, radio, recorders, and cameras have swept in within a matter of decades. People are adept listeners and viewers, but evidently poor readers and writers. So why all the concern with literacy?

The arguments put forth by literacy advocates strongly assert that illiterates, marginal literates, pseudoliterates, functional illiterates, aliterates, and nonliterates all live incomplete lives. They cannot participate fully in society's central processes. They are cut off, isolated, deprived. They are also a burden upon the enlightened, the literate. They cannot pay taxes but consume public resources; they make costly errors on their jobs; they cannot know "the issues" and therefore cannot vote intelligently. None of these assertions, however, is supported by hard evidence. Illiterates work. Illiterates pay taxes and vote. Illiterates may make mistakes because they are unable to read, but literates make similar mistakes when they misread, misinterpret, misunderstand, and misapply what they have read.

The deep concern for universal literacy stems from the assumption that reading and writing are essential for functioning in a modern world. Literacy, it is claimed, is a vital social and economic skill. Those who acquire it are enabled to enjoy all the benefits of the modern world; those who do not are destined to live lives of marginality.

All of this is, of course, far too general and simplistic. So, too, is the implication that universal literacy will solve all deprivation. Indeed, even the lesser suggestion that literacy is only part of the solution is too facile.

The "Function" of Literacy

Perhaps the quest for literacy became sidetracked when attention became focused on its functional applications. In less than a century literacy had been transformed from a means of faith and moral fortitude to a means of job security and career advancement. It ceased being the mark of an "educated person" and became a prerequisite for upward mobility. From being a value it became merely a skill. The literacy that nations pursue in their present public pronouncements is no longer the literacy of the past; it has been shorn of its transcendental qualities.

Professor Patricia A. Graham of Harvard University has described literacy thus:

> Literacy enhances our humanity. If we are literate in late twentieth century America, we expand the ways in which we can learn, understand, and appreciate the world around us. Through literacy we enlarge the range of our vicarious experience, both through our command of written materials and through formulation of new ideas demanded by the rigors of writing and speaking. . . . To learn, to express, to decide and to do . . . together permit us to become more autonomous individuals, less circumscribed by the conditions of social class, sex, and ethnicity into which we are born.[1]

Humanity, expansion, learning, understanding, appreciation, expression, mobility, autonomy: such concepts offer a vision in which literacy plays a crucial role, because they are concepts deeply embedded in the American psyche. Such goals can be met only through constant effort, part of which must entail a continuous quest for the attainment and development of literacy.

Literacy is freedom. Literacy makes it possible for people to determine for themselves what they wish to know, and in what depth; it enables people to transcend the boundaries set by others. The medieval objection to mass literacy was not anchored in the fear that people might read the Scriptures, but rather that they might, through reading them, arrive at conclusions unacceptable to the Church. Moreover, since literacy once acquired is not limited to one book, "uncontrolled" literacy could breed heretical literature, dangerous to the preservation of "the proper order." If all but the "trusted" are kept illiterate, the dangers of sedition influenced by a free flow of ideas can be held in check. Throughout history people in power have sought to control the written word. Book burnings, censorship, and the perpetuation of illiteracy have all been means to that end.

Democratic values depend on a free flow of information, with each individual assured the right—and the ability—to pursue any direction of thought and study. Clearly, democracy can only be sustained if divergent views and desires adhere to the notion of majority rule, determined by democratic processes and predicated on the free expression of ideas. In this scheme literacy is vital, for it alone makes possible the unfettered explorations that are the hallmarks of true independence.

Literacy is also memory. History and human experience are best preserved in writing. Cultures sustained through oral means are subject to transformation and loss. Many native American groups and descendants of nonliterate immigrants, almost entirely shorn of their cultural heritage, are painstakingly trying to recreate and regain it through arduous archeological explorations and visits to distant lands of origin. The search for roots is indicative of the need to connect with the past in order to better establish present identity.

Literacy gives one access to one's past and a continuity of identity. It is also a means to transfer past and present into the future. Parents provide their children, among other things, with identities that are firmly anchored in history—which is an extension of memory. Literacy makes it possible to retain that memory and pass it on to others.

Memory has other important uses. We live in a world in which important events occur daily. These events affect our lives, directly and indirectly. None occurs in a vacuum. They all have contexts that need to be understood. To some limited extent the electronic media try to provide context, but the accent must be placed on the word *limited*. Time constraints force the reduction of even the most momentous occurrences to their most basic facts. Full understanding of present events requires literacy, which make it possible, in greater leisure, to fill the canvas with all the necessary background and detail.

Literacy makes possible depth and breadth, the pursuit of inquiry in any direction. The illiterate must be satisfied with the knowledge supplied by others. They are prisoners of what is meted out, unable to pursue avenues of inquiry determined by themselves. Such inquiry in itself is a vital force in human development: it fuels invention and innovation, enabling the mind to expand and to reach into the future, guided by the accumulated records of the past.

Literacy is communication. Not just the communication made possible by television, radio, and telephones, but the exchange of thoughts, ideas, and knowledge across space and time. For literacy is not bound in time. It is portable, available for use whenever individuals are moved to read or write.

Far from being an anachronism, literacy remains one of humanity's finest and most important inventions, irreplaceable despite all the technological advances of our time. Without it we would remain in a state of subjugation, subject to the whims of the few who are literate. With it we are liberated, free, independent.

To be sure, literacy also has a multitude of functional applications. Many of those are not as real as some believe, and many have been replaced by other—not always more efficient—mechanisms. If we pursue universal literacy only because of its functional uses, we will not be successful. We will be guilty of neglecting literacy's main attributes and purposes. Literacy cannot be viewed merely as a "useful bag of tricks." If the goal of universal literacy is to be achieved, it has to be viewed as part of the unending quest for the attainment of those social and philosophical visions that underlie our civilization. Literacy is not just the ability to read: it is a fundamental component of our culture.

Literacy and Social Action

In America as elsewhere there are disadvantaged people. Public programs have sought to ameliorate the conditions of these people, to enable them to partake more fully in the bounties that the country has to offer. Many "quick fix" programs have been attempted; employing such devices as early childhood development activities, remedial instruction, and job training. A number of welfare programs seek to sustain life until such a time as these efforts will bear fruit. Literacy has been offered as one of the quick fixes. Many of its advocates argue that literacy has the power to liberate people from disadvantage by giving them the tools to obtain employment and advance up the job ladder. Experience has shown that the task is not as simple as one might like.

Disadvantage has multiple causes and does not lend itself to simple solutions. Panaceas don't exist. Difficult issues can be dealt with only by tackling the causal factors: economic conditions, housing, health, jobs, cultural values, community standards, personal attitudes. And even then success is not assured. Literacy might become only one aspect of social policy, and possibly not a central one. It might be found that literacy growth is a result, rather than a cause, of other advances. Changed conditions bring about changed motivations, and motivation is an essential in the acquisition of literacy.

It is far too simplistic to suggest that literacy can be spread universally through a blitz campaign. It is equally unrealistic to expect the illiterate to buy notions of literacy when other aspects of their lives do not support its acquisition. Literacy sown in barren fields will not grow; literacy planted in fertile and tended land will blossom. Lacking the proper conditions, artificial efforts will be frustrated.

It is said that there are waiting lists of those seeking literacy instruction, unable to obtain it because of lack of space and capacity. All that is required in order to solve the literacy problem, some argue, is a significant increase in classes, teachers, and, of course, funds. But those making the argument neglect to mention that fifty percent of the people who enter literacy programs leave before the programs have been completed and that the same proportion lapse back into illiteracy soon after "graduation." The issue, then, is not one of capacity but, of literacy readiness, a condition determined by the lives people lead, the atmosphere in which they function, the communities and families they belong to, and the culture that gives their lives meaning.

"Quick fixes" ultimately "fix" nothing. They ignore the complexities of what they attempt to rectify. This kind of approach has permeated literacy activities far too long, to the detriment of those who might have benefited from more appropriate efforts—and to the detriment of society as a whole.

Literacy can contribute to social well-being, but cannot create it. It cannot even serve as a harbinger of social betterment; it must be part of a process and will only take root when appropriate conditions are met.

A Smorgasbord of Literacies

Literacy, as we have seen, is not the same thing to all people at all times. It is not a fixed set of skills that, once acquired, becomes permanent. It is, instead, a concept that assumes different definitions in different places, at different times, as conditions warrant. Consequently, different contexts and groups evolve definitions of literacy that have a diversity of content and strive to inculcate those definitions among their members. In this regard literacy has amoebic qualities, constantly changing shape in response to need and challenges.

A meaningful definition of literacy is not merely a statement about the grade-level equivalence at which people ought to be able to read; literacy entails a notion of language and content. These, in turn, differ widely, depending on the contexts that establish and support them. In common parlance literacy has already assumed this attribute: we make reference to science literacy, economic literacy, consumer literacy, computer literacy. In each case the connotation of the term *literacy* is that of some basic acquirement deemed necessary. Without such notions of content, the basic skill of reading has virtually no meaning; with them reading abilities assume direction and purpose.

Literacy, then, is not merely the ability to decipher letters and assemble them into words. Nor is it a determination of a satisfactory level of comprehension. Literacy is a smorgasbord unique to each different table on which it is spread. It is a combination of technical skills that make it possible, with content and purpose, to interact with the specific environments in which people live and function.

For this reason it is erroneous to suggest that illiteracy is confined to those who cannot read. Illiteracy exists wherever there are people whose reading and writing skills are inadequate for the situation in which they find themselves. A class in "executive writing" is as much a literacy program as is a course in English as a second language or a program in which basic reading skills are imparted. In each case literacy is defined in accordance with contextual requirements and conditions.

Literacy and Community

The link between literacy and community is intimate and vital. A nationally derived definition of literacy would be inappropriate, for communities themselves must identify and define the literacies necessary for their members. And the communities are potentially the best vehicles for the spread of the literacy that they have defined.

Communities, of course, include workplaces, neighborhoods, religious groups, clubs, and organization of various types. While there has been recognition of the potential inherent in community groups, it has largely focused on their ability to serve as purveyors of literacy instruction. But many such groups around the country—at present their numbers are estimated to be upward of three thousand—erode their own inherent potential by seeking to copy from others a "best" curriculum or teaching method. By adopting programs that may be effective elsewhere but are not appropriate to local needs, community structures in effect become foreigners in their own bailiwicks, rendered incapable of achieving their objectives.

For communities to be able to develop and grow in accordance with their own specific attributes, it is necessary for the people developing community programs to heed the messages being broadcast locally, and not to search for programs developed elsewhere. Where technical assistance could be helpful is in identifying local needs and developing curricula and teaching methods suitable for those needs. Since literacy is intertwined with other community attributes, community programs seeking to promote it are best coordinated with other community programs.

Schools are among those community institutions whose function is greatly enhanced when they relate to the communities they serve.

Most don't. They seek, instead, to teach a curriculum that is more or less universal and for that reason has mixed results. For schools to function effectively, they need the kind of support that emanates from the trust and acceptance of the community. When they are perceived as foreign implants, schools simply cannot be effective in carrying out their missions. Fully integrated into their communities they can be a powerful force for change and growth. In isolation they can achieve little. United with other efforts aimed at adult members of communities, they can help break age-old cycles of illiteracy.

Each community has to develop its own means—formal and informal—to inculcate literacy. Interlocking communities can also exert influence on one another through members who simultaneously belong to several. Coordinated effort is required, not the "single-shot" type of activities that have generally characterized literacy programs. If what occurs in one community is supported within that community and in other communities with overlapping membership, the combined efforts can yield impressive results.

The spread of literacy is not primarily a pedagogic challenge. It is above all a mission that requires integrated strategy and policy, accompanied by educational activities well grounded in precepts of adult learning and anchored in community structures.

Action and Research

Despite statements regarding the adequacy of current knowledge about literacy and instruction, the fact remains that solid research on the subject is virtually nil. Studies whose conclusions might provide guidance are few and far between. Since the general attitude towards literacy has for a long time been that the issue is a temporary one, little energy has been expended on improving our understanding of its intricacies. Hypotheses abound—all unexamined. So intellectually impoverished is the area of literacy studies that it cannot seem to attract the sustained attention of the research community. As a result, practice navigates its own course and, more often than not, flounders.

Illiteracy is probably a permanent issue. No sooner does a group of people become literate than the definition of literacy is likely to change, setting new objectives and requiring further development of instruction techniques. It is in the nature of humankind that new heights are continuously sought; new futures supplant tried pasts. Literacy does not remain static throughout these movements; it is constantly modified and redefined in order to follow and facilitate them. If, indeed, this pattern is understood and can supplant the current notion that illiteracy is a poison and literacy acquisition its antidote, then it must logically follow that in-depth research is essential.

Research is an activity that seeks to unlock elusive secrets and discover new insights in order to deepen and broaden our understanding of phenomena. There has unfortunately been so little research undertaken into matters pertaining to literacy that most of its secrets await discovery. In the absence of such research future efforts will have the same trial-and-error nature as present ones—with the same frustrations.

Some of literacy's staunchest advocates are themselves illiterate in the area of adult education. Slogans, unsubstantiated assertions, simplistic analyses, and feelings of righteousness do not abrogate the need to understand the problem. Such a posture is inimical to the very goals that literacy advocates hold dear. It is also a posture that appears to neglect the very essence of literacy itself.

This is not a plea to stop literacy programs until all the central questions have been answered. It is, rather, a reminder that the quest for literacy, if it is to be successful, must be guided by understanding, research, and experience.

Literacy Consciousness

An aspect of literacy that has perhaps not been adequately emphasized is that literacy skills are only as valuable as the uses to which they are put. Universal literacy—itself an elusive goal—is not equivalent to universal reading. Unapplied and unutilized literacy abilities alone have no intrinsic value.

The task of achieving a fully literate society—one in which reading and writing are natural and common human activities—transcends the task of teaching reading and writing to everyone. Literacy is a value, not a skill. The challenge facing us is that of establishing literacy as a universal, permanent, basic value in American life. Literate people tend to believe that it already is. Let us hope that they are right. But there is increasing evidence, as this book has tried to show, that literacy is becoming less and less regarded as a necessary or even desirable achievement. The neglect of reading by literate people is as much of a tragedy as the failure to attain universal literacy, and is potentially more serious. Unless this trend is reversed, there is little hope of inducing more people to acquire reading skills. The challenge is to civilization itself.

The problem of generating literacy consciousness poses a challenge possibly greater than that of teaching literacy. It is one that has never been squarely faced and about which even less is known than the problem of illiteracy. The numbers of people who are capable of reading but don't is as baffling a problem as the numbers of people who are unable to read. It is certainly possible that the two phenomena are linked: nonreading literates certainly do not inspire illiterates to acquire reading habits.

Policy, programs, and research should all begin grappling with the fundamental issue of literacy activity, in addition to their preoccupation with illiteracy. Dealing with the latter and neglecting the former is not unlike the road gang that set out to pave a road to a thriving neighboring town, only to discover when they finally arrived that it no longer existed.

A Postliterate Age?

It has been suggested that we are entering a postliterate age. This may be true, provided that a postliterate age is understood as one in which literacy is no longer the one major medium of communication. As Marshall McLuhan pointed out a generation ago, the introduction of electronic media has altered human perception in a way that is irreversible.

But if a postliterate age is viewed as one in which literacy is doomed to disappear, then that age has not arrived—literacy is as vital as ever it was, if not more so. One of the purposes of this book is to point the way to a course of action that will maintain that vitality.

The opinion has been put forth, seemingly as a middle ground, that literacy is no longer a skill required of the masses—that it is gradually becoming confined to those elites who need it and can make use of it. It is important, this argument runs, that *access* to literacy should be universal, so that those with the ability and desire to acquire it may do so, while the others—presumably the majority—can knowingly reject it. Such an argument is an abhorrent throwback to the Middle Ages. It underscores, however, the great importance of understanding why it is that so many choose not to read, what that reflects about the current state of American cultures, and how the task of instilling literacy consciousness can be approached. A non-reading society is an impoverished one. For a society that has already achieved impressive strides towards universal literacy, abandoning the quest would be a regression—and a cause for great concern. There is in this direction a potential for degeneration.

The problem of illiteracy can be seen as a classic dilemma—a choice between two equally unsatisfactory choices, each of which seems to rule out the other. If we plunge in without taking time to study the problem our efforts will be useless and possibly harmful; if we take the time to study it, the problem may deteriorate beyond our ability to solve it before we have devised a solution.

Fortunately, the choices need not be that extreme. While the "quick fix" approach is not going to solve the basic problem, the enthusiasm this approach has generated indicates the widespread concern for the attainment of universal literacy, and such concern is vital if change is to be brought about. As we pointed out in Chapter 6, many benefits have resulted from the various adult literacy programs, even though the problem of instilling literacy consciousness has yet to be solved.

And while the other horn of the dilemma—taking time to study the problem—seems to postpone a solution for an unreasonable length of time, it must be remembered that the problem is in the process of being solved while the study is being done. For example, many people's lives have been saved as a result of the continuing research on cancer, although the problem of cancer itself is yet to be completely solved. Similarly, the causes of illiteracy can be dealt with—and are being dealt with—as more becomes known about them, although full understanding of this complex problem may take years. What is important, and what this book has stressed repeatedly, is that to solve the problem we must know the causes. Action uninformed by knowledge leads nowhere.

What Action?

Literacy has been presented throughout this book as a variable and relative set of abilities rather than as a fixed set of skills. We have argued that multiple definitions of literacy exist, each deriving from unique circumstances and environments, and that definitions change in response to altered conditions and aspirations. A definition of literacy appropriate for one group of people is not necessarily either appropriate or viable for another.

These assertions have some important implications for the design of strategies to promote literacy. First, illiteracy has to be addressed in the contexts within which it occurs and not through a national program or nationwide curricula that are insensitive to different group and environmental characteristics. Programs should be designed for specific groups based on the situations, needs, and desires of their members. This clearly places the responsibility for program design and delivery on the shoulders of communities themselves. Community-based organizations, the workplace, churches and synagogues, local schools, community centers, and libraries are all agencies that could be excellent vehicles for literacy programs—and in very many instances they are already active. The kind of assistance that is required and should be made available, beyond financial support, is technical guidance in aspects of program design, curriculum and materials development, and training. Such support, however, should focus on the processes involved in each of these aspects and not attempt to offer "packaged" curricula and instructional approaches. Doing so would defeat the purpose of customizing programs to suit local conditions.

A second implication is that literacy programs are not "one-shot" efforts. They ought to be permanent activities that seek on a sustained basis to assist people in attaining the skills and knowledge they require and are motivated to attain at different times. The dynamic quality of literacy, coupled with the fact that definitions and needs change constantly, make this essential.

Literacy programs in this sense should be synonymous with adult education. Throughout the country, in many settings, as we have seen, this approach is fast becoming reality. Workplace education and training programs and the plethora of adult education activities being offered are examples of this trend. Policy should recognize this revolutionary change in the nature of education and provide the necessary supports. These include the sponsorship of research and development activities, the development of cadres of professionals at all levels, the creation of necessary linkages with other components of the education system, as well as with the world of work, and the creation of appropriate infrastructures. Adult education, intimately linked with changing literacies and definitions of literacy, has become an integral part of the life span. Educational policies should reflect this development.

Third, literacy programs directed at socially and economically disadvantaged groups must be fully coordinated with other efforts to improve the conditions of their members. Literacy alone cannot produce the desired changes. Literacy coupled with other interventions has a chance. At present, efforts are largely uncoordinated, to the detriment of all programs and, more importantly, to the detriment of those involved. It must be borne in mind that the children of families and environments that do not value and support literacy and education are severely handicapped in their own quest for learning and likely to become the next generation of illiterates. By coordinating efforts at teaching adults with those directed at children it might be possible to generate the supports and reinforcements that are so important for learning. Children and their parents stand to benefit.

One suggestion put forth and widely touted has been that illiteracy can be "solved" through a combination of recruiting armies of teachers—volunteers and professionals—and pouring massive amounts of money into financing a blitz campaign. Literacy development is an ongoing process that can only be effective if programs are very carefully designed to meet the requirements of specific groups of participants. Literacy development can only begin to take root when individuals are properly motivated. Literacy teachers require specialized skills and sensibilities, in turn requiring substantial training. "Quick fix" campaigns are not geared to any of these. Their records around the world are poor: drop-out is inordinately high and retention of skills extremely low. As mentioned above, such approaches ultimately "fix" nothing. They generate a great deal of activity, promote an atmosphere of crisis, engage many people—but in the end contribute very little to rectification of the issue itself.

The strategy suggested in this book proposes a very carefully planned, long-term, and sustained instructional effort focused on groups of people within their communities of affiliation and based on constant analysis of their circumstances, needs, and motivations. It offers the antithesis to the "quick fix" approach—an adult education effort with a changing curriculum that would become a permanent part of peoples' lives, available as an aid to the continued growth and development made necessary by constantly changing conditions and definitions of literacy. Such a system of education has become an imperative of our time: anything less cannot properly address the central literacy-related dilemmas society faces.

NOTES

Chapter One

1. William S. Gray, *The Teaching of Reading and Writing,* Monographs on Fundamental Education, No. 10, UNESCO (Paris: 1956), p. 24.
2. Carman St. John Hunter and David Harman, *Adult Illiteracy in the United States: A Report to the Ford Foundation* (New York: McGraw Hill, 1979), pp. 7–8.

Chapter Two

1. Eric Havelock, *The Origins of Western Literacy,* Toronto: Ontario Institute for Studies of Education, 1976, p. 12.
2. Jack Goody and Ian Watt, "The Consequences of Literacy," in Jack Goody (editor), *Literacy in Traditional Societies* (Cambridge: Cambridge University Press, 1968), pp. 27, 28.
3. Alexander Calloway, in E. P. Thompson, *The Making of the English Working Class* (Middlesex: Penguin, 1965), p. 717.
4. Carlo M. Cipolla, *Literacy and Development in the West* (Middlesex: Penguin, 1969), p. 88.
5. Gunnar Myrdal, *Asian Drama* (New York: Pantheon, 1968), Vol. 3, p. 1667.
6. Julius Nyerere, Address to Parliament on the Inauguration of the First Five Year Development Plan (May 1964).
7. Lawrence Cremin, "Reading, Writing, and Literacy," *Review of Education* (1975, no. 1).

Chapter Three

1. Anthony P. Carnevale, "The Learning Enterprise," *Training and Development Journal* (January 1986).
2. Sylvia Scribner and Michael Cole, *The Psychology of Literacy* (Cambridge: Harvard University Press, 1981).
3. John Roueche, *Salvage, Redirection or Custody? Remedial Education in the Junior College* (Washington: American Associate of Community Colleges), 1968
4. John Roueche, "Literacy Needs and Development in American Community Colleges" (Paper presented at the National Adult Literacy Conference, Washington, 1984).

Chapter Four

1. *What Works: Research About Teaching and Learning* (Washington: U.S. Department of Education, 1986).

Chapter Five

1. *What Works: Research About Teaching and Learning* (Washington: U.S. Department of Education, 1986).
2. Stephen Graubard, Introduction to special issue on adulthood, *Daedalus* (Spring 1976).
3. Benjamin Bloom, *Stability and Change in Human Characteristics* (Chicago: Aldine, 1964).
4. Allen H. Tough, *The Adult's Learning Projects* (Toronto: Ontario Institute for Studies in Education, 1971).

Chapter Seven

1. Patricia A. Graham, "Literacy: A Goal for Secondary Schools," *Daedalus* (Summer 1981).

INDEX